HilaryDuff

Hilary Duff

All Access

By Matthew Rettenmund

Photography by Keith Munyan

BERKLEY BOULEVARD BOOKS, NEW YORK

THE BERKLEY PUBLISHING GROUP
Published by the Penguin Group
Penguin Group (USA) Inc.
375 Hudson Street, New York, New York 10014, USA
Penguin Group (Canada), 10 Alcorn Avenue, Toronto, Ontario M4V 3B2, Canada
(a division of Pearson Penguin Canada Inc.)
Penguin Books Ltd., 80 Strand, London WC2R 0RL, England
Penguin Group Ireland, 25 St. Stephen's Green, Dublin 2, Ireland (a division of Penguin Books Ltd.)
Penguin Group (Australia), 250 Camberwell Road, Camberwell, Victoria 3124, Australia
(a division of Pearson Australia Group Pty. Ltd.)
Penguin Books India Pvt. Ltd., 11 Community Centre, Panchsheel Park, New Delhi—110 017, India
Penguin Group (NZ), Cnr. Airborne and Rosedale Roads, Albany, Auckland 1310, New Zealand
(a division of Pearson New Zealand Ltd.)
Penguin Books (South Africa) (Pty.) Ltd., 24 Sturdee Avenue, Rosebank, Johannesburg 2196,
South Africa

Penguin Books Ltd., Registered Offices: 80 Strand, London WC2R 0RL, England

This book is an original publication of The Berkley Publishing Group.

The publisher does not have any control over and does not assume any responsibility for author or third-party
websites or their content.

PRINTING HISTORY
Berkley Boulevard trade paperback edition / July 2005

Library of Congress Cataloging-in-Publication Data

Rettenmund, Matthew.
    Hilary Duff: all access / by Matthew Rettenmund ; photography by Keith Munyan.
        p. cm.
    ISBN 0-425-20519-3
    1. Duff, Hilary, 1987– 2. Singers—United States—Biography. I. Title.

ML420.D915R47 2005
792.02'8'092—dc22

                                                         2005041089

PRINTED IN THE UNITED STATES OF AMERICA

10   9   8   7   6   5   4   3   2   1

Hilary Duff

Hair!

Makeup!

Feed the dog!

All set!

The cover look is complete!

Introduction

The Real Hilary Duff!

What is Hilary Duff really like?

As the editor of *Popstar!* magazine, I can guarantee this is the first question someone will ask me when they find out what I do. Children, teenagers, parents—there seem to be no boundaries to Hilary Duff's fan base.

I first met Hilary in the spring of 2001. Earlier that year, a publicist at Disney Channel had offered to send one of my staffers to Disney's California Adventure on the West Coast to spend a day at the then-new park with the stars of some of her network's fledgling shows: Hilary Duff (*Lizzie McGuire*), Shia LaBeouf (*Even Stevens*), and Kyla Pratt (*The Proud Family*). She returned with high praise for all three—and to her credit, each has gone on to great success!—but she had a special affection for the blond girl from Texas who had good-naturedly allowed herself to get doused on a water ride, helped bake a cake for her mom, and attracted tons of attention even then, when only the first couple of episodes of *Lizzie McGuire* had aired. The photographer reported that the camera loved Hilary—and the results were later published in the August 2001 issue of *Popstar!*, Hilary's first major spread (including a pinup) in a teen magazine.

My co-worker's enthusiasm set off my pop-culture radar. In the past, I'd been the first editor to put 98° on the cover of a magazine, I'd been the first journalist ever to interview Jessica Simpson, and *Popstar!* had scored early coverage of everyone from Lindsay Lohan to Chad Michael Murray. Hilary Duff, for whatever reason, just sounded *right.* Even before I met her in person, I scheduled an exclusive photo shoot with Hilary in New York City.

At a Thirty-ninth Street photography studio, on June 13, 2001, we were shooting an outrageous European band just before Hilary arrived. For teen-entertainment magazines, once an editor identifies an act that will have extended appeal, it makes sense to pay for a photo shoot to have various looks to run over the course of several issues. This particular day found us cutting it *really* close!

The Euro group, today just a pop-music memory, was taking a long

Hilary as she appeared in one of the first frames ever snapped of her by Keith Munyan!

time between looks. I was totally embarrassed when the band was in the middle of changing outfits right in the open just as the Duffs arrived. Major oops! I was worried that Hilary and her mom, Susan, might storm out in shock. Instead, they laughed and waited their turn for Hilary to pose for my photographer. They chitchatted with me in their inimitably bubbly way and introduced me to the professional who did Hilary's hair and makeup in the early years of her career, a family friend.

Immediately, I adored Hilary. In person, Hilary is just as pretty as in pictures. As corny as it sounds, she has a glow that comes from her heart. She's also incredibly funny and fun-loving—she even did cartwheels around our studio! Unlike many of her peers, Hilary Duff at that age and even now refuses to behave beyond her years. She's mature enough to engage in business decisions (and to fulfill any and all obligations even when she's pooped), but she cherishes being a teenager and leaves herself plenty of time to be a normal kid.

During the shoot, Hilary wore a camouflage outfit (shades of her future TV hit *Cadet Kelly*), a white tank, and a T-shirt with "Juicy 00" written on it. She was such a major Juicy Couture fan that Hilary was nicknamed Juicy Fruit by her friends. Inexperienced in front of the camera except for a few small, internal Disney Channel promo shoots, Hilary quickly became comfortable projecting her personality as the photographer clicked away.

That first photo shoot with Hilary Duff was one of the very few times I have watched a relatively unknown performer who I was absolutely certain would become a superstar.

The camera, one of Hilary's first and biggest fans, would later help seal an enduring friendship between the Duffs and Keith Munyan, another longtime *Popstar!* photographer who I assigned to shoot Hilary in 2002 in Los Angeles. From the moment they met, Keith has been Hilary's favorite photographer, and he has captured all the very best images of the teen phenom. Keith's amazing images appear regularly in teen magazines. His photographs fill this book and are the images Hilary's fans most associate with their idol.

Since my first encounter with Hilary, our paths have crossed many times—I've had lunch with her at Planet Hollywood Times Square in New York City, traveled to Hawaii with her for her TV special, attended her Radio Disney concert in Los Angeles, and tracked her movements as she's made movies and recorded albums. I've seen her go from *Popstar!* to *Vanity Fair* and launch a personal brand that ranks with Mary-Kate and Ashley Olsen's.

Through it all, I've admired Hilary not only as an entertainer but as a delightful human being—a truly good person—and it was my goal that this book be the ultimate tribute to the girl herself, to her fans (good taste!), and to the ideals she stands for: hard work, fun times, and caring about the world.

Enjoy!

MRettermy.

January 2005

So Yesterday

Hilary's Life Story!

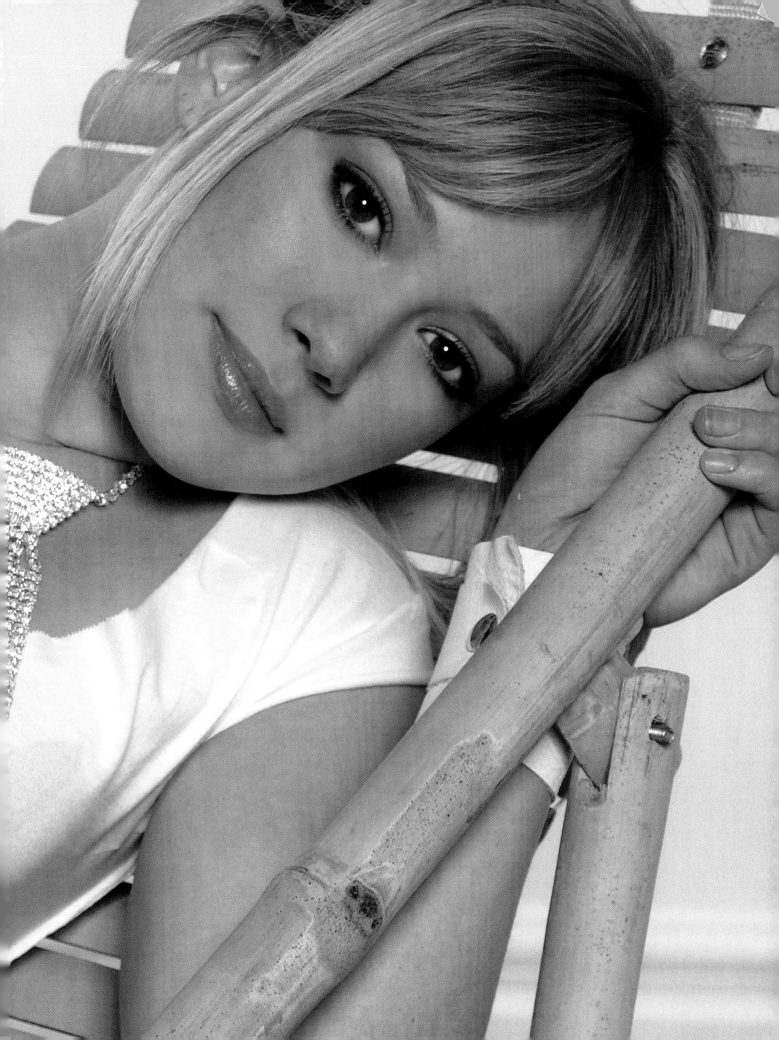

Anywhere but Here: A Star Is Born

For her fans, it may be hard to remember a time before Hilary Duff was a household name—but it wasn't all that long ago!

Hilary was born Monday, September 28, 1987, to Bob and Susan Duff. She would spend the earliest part of her childhood in Houston, but the Duffs also owned a historically important ranch in nearby Bastrop. Contrary to rumors that her middle name might be Ann or Lisa, Hilary was actually given the unusual middle name of Erhard, which was Bob's mother, Mary's, maiden name. Naming Hilary after her was a tribute to the locally powerful and respected Erhard family. Adolph Erhard had arrived in Bastrop, Texas, from Munich, Germany, in 1840, which means Hilary is a sixth-generation Texan. Other prominent Erhards had founded the First National Bank of Bastrop and operated the Home Hardware Store—Hilary's great-great-grandfather was even dubbed Mr. Bastrop County!

Speaking of family matters, family *matters* to Hilary Duff! As most of her fans know, Hilary was the second child Bob and Susan had—she followed older sister, Haylie Katherine (born Tuesday, February 19, 1985), who would become a major influence for Hilary and even an artistic collaborator later in life!

Mom Susan sold cosmetics and Dad Bob co-owned a huge chain called Timewise Food Stores in the Houston area. Well liked by their neighbors, the Duffs were always a tight-knit family whose deep roots in Texas were reflected in their involvement in the Bastrop and Houston communities.

Susan Duff recalled a traditional upbringing for Hilary to *Cowboys & Indians* magazine, saying that the Duffs would show up at the Family Fair at the Annual Livestock Show and Rodeo and dances at Gruene Hall near New Braunfels, Texas. "Everybody was dancing—kids standing on their parents' feet learning to two-step."

Both Hilary and Haylie were physically active. Susan has even called Hilary a tomboy of sorts, considering she adored "swimming a mile," rollerblading, climbing trees, and gymnastics.

As well-behaved as Hilary seems today, she wasn't *always* that way! She told *Popstar!* in 2001 that she was a little willful as a child—so much so that time-outs didn't even work on her!

"I used to talk back a lot when I was a little kid," Hilary confessed.

When given time-outs, Hilary related that she'd play with toys in her room or pick at wallpaper in the bathroom or hallway—there was no way to keep her still as a form of punishment! "My fingers were always busy!"

Susan recognized very early on that both of her daughters—one by one—were drawn to dancing and acting.

Hilary would later tell *YM* magazine, "Ever since I was five, my sister and I used to watch TV and then we'd turn it off and act out the scenes together. Haylie would say, 'Since you have short hair and I have long, pretty hair, you have to be the boy.' She was evil!"

Haylie was the fearless trailblazer, appearing in school productions and exploring ballet by the age of eight.

"At home, she would teach me all these dances," Hilary later remembered, "and then I wanted to start doing them, too."

The girls were learning the Cecchetti method of ballet, a strict and classical system that encourages students to think of their bodies' movements as one unified piece of motion. Balance and strength are honed in this form of ballet, and the durable Duffs excelled.

When Hilary made what has been called her stage debut, in a touring company of the BalletMet Columbus production of *The Nutcracker*, she was only six years old. Hilary relished all the eyes on her, and the approval for a job well done. She was, after all, the little girl who idolized her sister and begged to wear red shoes every day at age three because they were the prettiest and got the most attention!

Unlike some siblings, there was never any rivalry between the Duff girls, only mutual admiration and support.

"'Please' and 'thank you' were probably some of the first words my kids learned," Susan Duff has said, illustrating the loving and unbreakable bond she and Bob were instilling between their daughters. This early training in courtesy was further hammered home by Susan's longstanding devotion to charitable work. She would throw elaborate holiday parties, but insist guests make donations instead of bringing gifts.

"Texas, to me, is all about that—family and friends, and courtesy," Hilary told *Cowboys & Indians*.

I recall one time giving Susan a funny rhinestone "The Mom" pin and giving Hilary a trinket from a popular on-line store. Susan waved them off, saying, "We don't need anything, Matthew. With the Duffs, gifts are not required."

The Duff sisters were, and are, a team. They have always looked out for each other, and they generously inspired each other in their dreams of performing.

Susan Duff would do anything for her daughters! That's why she agreed to take them to Los Angeles to become performers—and that's why she has said she would support them if they called it quits!

Quiz!
Were You Born to Be a Star?

Some people were born to be famous—their destiny is written in the stars (so to speak)! Others have to work hard to achieve a measure of success. Still others make better fans than idols.

Are you someone fated to become a legend in your own time . . . or are you a legend in your own mind? Take this quiz and discover your destiny . . . if you dare!

Which activities more closely mirror your own favorite hobbies?

A. Baby-sitting, going to the movies, and talking on the phone with friends!

B. Trying out for school plays, playing dress-up, and inventing stage names for yourself!

How do you feel about your favorite stars?

A. "I could never be in their shoes . . . how on earth do they do it?"

B. "If someone gave me a shot, I could do just as well!"

C. "I truly admire their talents and I understand exactly what they did to develop them!"

Which list of skills better reflects your own greatest gifts?

A. Spelling, math, and science!

B. Singing, dancing, and acting!

Do you ever feel guilty if you've spent a day being unproductive?

A. No way! Breaks are essential and vacations are A-okay!

B. Actually, yeah. If I'm not being creative, I feel lazy!

What type of person do you more strongly consider yourself to be?

A. A total wallflower—someone who doesn't even like to meet new people, let alone go to a party!

B. An outgoing social butterfly who enjoys new situations and making lots of new friends!

You're asked to speak at a large gathering about a cause you passionately support. What are you probably gonna do?

A. Politely refuse because being the center of attention is something you're still getting used to!

B. Accept the challenge and buy a new outfit to make sure you'll look your best!

C. Memorize your speech, study up so you can easily take questions afterward and send an e-mail blast to all your friends asking them to come!

The Fame Scale

0   **1**   **2**   **3**   **4**

The Fame Scale!

0

Don't feel bad, but you may not have the right personality type for the fame game. It's not out of the question for you, but you may want to focus instead on your personal happiness rather than on trying to make millions of people around the world happy!

1

The cards are stacked against you becoming superfamous, mainly because you lack the crazy drive that's needed. You have talent and energy, but you don't want fame badly enough to pursue it. Decide now if it's something you crave. If not, it won't come knocking!

2

You definitely have a spark in you that some people refer to as an X factor. People notice you and appreciate your personality and your abilities. With only a little more effort, you might just find yourself on the cover of a magazine someday!

3

You may have great talent and you probably have an inordinate amount of drive. You're not afraid to do what it takes to succeed, though you might at times be more interested in being famous than being famous for your unique talents. Buckle down and you are heading for the big-time, baby!

4

You have the personality type that will help take you to the top, and your remarkable talent will keep you there. Rather than shallowly pursuing notoriety, your consummate skills and your love of your creative expression (art, singing, dancing) will make you known far and wide!

Eventually, the girls' love of the stage led Susan to relocate them to San Antonio. Most of Hilary's later childhood was spent there on their ranch. A few years ago, when asked by a teen magazine to spill one secret about herself that no one knew, Hilary said, "I grew up on a ranch in San Antonio, Texas!"

Hilary did like performing, but she didn't *always* want to be a famous actress and singer. "When I was a little girl, I didn't think this is what I wanted to do," she candidly said during an MSN chat in 2002. Becoming a star wasn't Hilary's dream at first, but . . . let's just say it was a sister thing!

"When we moved to San Antonio from Houston, we went to a performing arts school," Hilary recalled in 2001. "We did a lot of plays and dances and stuff. My sister started doing it, so of course I had to start doing it—everything she does, I do!"

The girls were fortunate enough to be attending the prestigious St. Mary's Hall, founded in 1879 and known for its arts program.

As for where her dedication to the *art* of acting came from, Hilary has told the story many times, and it always begins with Haylie!

"It all kind of started with my sister!" Hilary emphatically told a teen-magazine reporter. "My sister actually was doing *Romeo and Juliet* and she didn't want to be bad in front of her friends—she wanted to do a really good job because she had a lead role in it. There was a little acting workshop near our house that she started to go to. When my mom asked me if I wanted to go, I thought it was so stupid and I would *never* want to do that. My sister kept coming home and showing me all the stuff she learned and I was like, 'Mom, I want to do that.' So I just kind of followed in Haylie's footsteps."

It's no surprise that the Duffs allowed their young daughters access to an acting workshop at a time when other parents might discourage the expense and the distraction from school. Karen Bradford of HowToBeAStar.com, who's known the family from their earliest days in Los Angeles, says, "Susan . . . is an instrumental force in their lives. She taught them that when you have something to do, you do a good job. That is why Hilary and Haylie are where they are today. Susan made sure that they were prepared. If they needed to be coached, they were coached."

No one in Hilary and Haylie's family had ever had artistic aspirations before them, but the girls' enthusiasm fed on itself as they excitedly compared notes on what they were learning at school. They pushed their mom and at first she didn't know what to make of their amazing drive.

"My husband and I were never involved in anything artistic," Susan told *Rolling Stone* in 2003, "so it was never anything we focused on."

Little Hilary's acting instruction seemed to do the trick—she landed her first TV appearance in a commercial for a local Texas cable company in which a dad runs in to tell his family they were wired for cable. Hilary's only line? "Do we get Disney Channel?" Who knew that just a few years later, Hilary would be the biggest star in Disney Channel's stable?

Over time, swayed by a trickle of paying acting jobs around Texas for the girls and by her daughters' concerted powers of persuasion, Susan made the momentous decision to take Hilary and Haylie to Los Angeles to see just how difficult it would be to break them in to acting. They left and took up temporary digs to brave their first pilot season, a short period of a few months when producers cast for television-show pilots that will be shopped to the networks.

At first, the Duffs felt they were leading charmed lives!

Quizzed in 2004 by Taylor Hanson for *Interview* magazine, Hilary remembered that first excursion to the Left Coast. "We first came out to California when I was six, and we booked commercials. We were like, 'This is easy!'" They returned to Texas full of hope—and "hope" was the operative word!

Around this time, Haylie landed a tiny role in Goldie Hawn's directorial debut, the made-for-TV movie *Hope*. Filmed in Texas, the movie gave the elder Duff daughter a taste of Hollywood without having to leave home!

In 1996, thanks to a lucky family connection, she and Hilary filmed appearances as extras in the acclaimed Hallmark Entertainment TV miniseries *True Women*. Starring Dana Delany, Rachael Leigh Cook, and Tina Majorino (who would later costar with Haylie in *Napoleon Dynamite!*), *True Women* was filmed partly in Hills Prairie, Texas, at a two-story home from 1852 that Hilary's grandparents, Ken and Mary, owned and had restored twenty-five years earlier.

According to no less an authority than Susan Duff herself, this experience gave the girls an eyeful of the entertainment business—and helped to fuel their interest in acting.

These run-ins with the world of Hollywood plus more commercial work led the family to believe Los Angeles was the ticket. Susan paid an agent one thousand dollars to help relocate them to L.A. and to lock down more work for the girls. Despite her good intentions, it was that rarest of occasions, a time when Susan's usually infallible instincts failed her. The woman they'd paid took the money and ran, leaving the Duffs feeling badly burned. They returned to Texas in defeat—momentarily.

"You audition and you don't get anything," Hilary told Taylor Hanson of that time period. Still, the Duffs don't give up easily—or at all. "I knew I wanted to act, and I was really driven, so I kept going."

Susan approached their strikeout rationally, intellectually. She bought up every resource she could lay her hands on, studying up on the business

Hilary

Hilary's dad, Bob, has
stayed in the background
of his daughters' careers,
but he's a central part of
their lives. In person, Bob
is the strong, silent type
with a wicked sense of
humor. He's definitely a
fun dad!

part of show business, learning all she could about management, about what agents do, and about how to be competitive in pilot season.

Armed with much more decisive knowledge of the uphill battle the Duff girls faced, Susan explained to Hilary and Haylie that if they truly wanted to try, try again, it would mean a lot of rejections, and she made sure they understood that not getting a part did *not* have to be the end of the world.

Journeying back and forth between San Antonio and Los Angeles, the Duffs went on every audition under the sun. Susan knew about every part that could possibly call for girls their age and physical description, and she made sure both Duff daughters were seen by every casting agent who would have a look. People who encountered the trio at the time recall Susan cold-calling in some cases, earnestly pitching the two adorable Texan girls she had to offer.

For many children, this kind of emotional roller coaster might be devastating. But Hilary, whose expectations were always realistic thanks to Susan's heart-to-hearts, didn't sweat the small stuff.

"I always loved the challenge of seeing how far you can get," she coolly told *Teen Vogue* in 2004. Nail-biting auditions? No problem.

Susan's stick-to-it-iveness finally stuck. Haylie was cast as Gina Adams in the straight-to-video release *Addams Family Reunion*, alongside famous stars Daryl Hannah, Tim Curry, Ray Walston, and Ed Begley Jr.

At the same time, Hilary went up for a part as Wendy the Witch in a planned video called *Casper Meets Wendy*, a sequel to the popular Christina Ricci film *Casper*. The part was huge—it was a lead!—so Hilary didn't get her hopes up, even though she was physically perfect to play the sweet sorceress with the sugary disposition.

After auditioning for *Casper Meets Wendy*, and after Haylie completed her latest job, the girls returned to San Antonio and took solace in school, hanging out with their friends, and playing with their beloved family pooch, Little Dog, a fox terrier/Chihuahua mix they'd had as far back as they could remember.

But their run of bad luck was about to magically change.

"My best friend and I were in the bathroom playing with makeup and my mom came upstairs," Hilary told *Life Story* magazine. "She said, 'Get packed. We're going to California!'"

Haylie Duff: Hilary's Dynamite Sis!

If Haylie Duff had been a science whiz or math buff, there is a very good chance the world would never have heard of her sister, Hilary. Everything Hay did, Hil wanted to do—and that admiration led both into entertainment careers.

For the first part of Hilary's career, when she was just becoming known, Haylie was often a mystery. Fans knew that she was a member of a girl group called Trilogy and that she had acting aspirations of her own (a 2003 pilot called *Alexander the Great* generated buzz but is now ancient history), but little else.

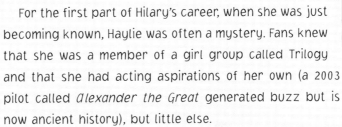

Over time, Haylie has emerged from the shadows and often makes appearances with her little sister, whether it's to help her feed McDonald's french fries to Latin singing legend Alejandro Fernandez for World Children's Day (as she did in November of 2004) or to help judge a best legs contest for Gillette at the *Good Morning America* studios in Times Square. More importantly, she duetted with Hilary on "The Siamese Cat Song" and on *A Cinderella Story*'s fun soundtrack song "Our Lips Are Sealed."

She's also a talented songwriter who's contributed unforgettable tracks to Hilary's albums.

Haylie told *USA Today* that being a Duff "doesn't make it easier or harder" to succeed. Her greatest success so far has been starring as bad girl Summer Wheatley in the massive 2004 indie hit *Napoleon Dynamite* and her fans cannot wait to see more of her when she and Hilary team up in the feature film *Material Girls,* due out in 2006. Hilary assessed her sister's abilities as a comedienne in *Teen Vogue*: "Haylie is really funny. Her comedic timing is crazy."

In person, Haylie is even more striking than in photos. She's got an aura of cool about her—it's no wonder her little sister used to worship the ground she walked on. These days, the sisters are on equal footing and are, by all accounts, best friends and confidantes.

"We don't go out for the same stuff," Haylie told *USA Today.* "We did when we were younger, but not anymore. We don't compete with each other—we're family."

I spoke with Haylie in Hawaii and also by phone after meeting her. I found her to be so much fun, so sweet, and such a future star in her own right.

Matthew: *You covered Hil's TV special as a correspondent for* Access Hollywood . . . *how was it?*

Haylie: Cool! I never really thought about doing anything on that side of the camera, but I got to follow Hilary around with my own little camera. I talked with Lauree Dash from *Access Hollywood*, who was helping me, and I was like, "I wanna be a reporter!"

Matthew: *You're a natural!*

Haylie: We've been around a lot of reporters so I guess I just referred to that!

Matthew: *What was the most fun you had on Kauai covering Hilary's special?*

Haylie: Probably the concert. I got to talk to my sister a little bit about performing and how she felt and I got to interview her. She worked so hard on that and put in so many rehearsals. She was really nervous before, too, so it was nice to see all her work pay off. Everybody knew all the words to her songs—and the album was only out for like *four days!*

Matthew: *How did you come to write the (awesome) track "Sweet Sixteen"?*

Haylie: Hilary wanted a song that was gonna talk about the freedom she was gonna get with turning sixteen, without sounding like she was all the way grown-up—just a light little song about turning sixteen.

   We did the music ten times—over and over and over again, and finally once we got it to the spot where it is now we were like, "Okay—that's it!"

Matthew: *It has a great '80s pop/punk sound!*

Haylie: Yeah! Like a driving song. We wanted the beginning to sound like opening a music box, that tinkling. That was always my sister and I's favorite thing—we always had a music box with a ballerina that turned in the middle.

Matthew: *You're a great songwriter—have you always written?*

Haylie: I started writing poems and then I realized I could turn poems into songs. So I wrote the song and I brought it to Hilary, and I was like, "Hil, I wrote a song for your album," and she was like, "Okay . . . wait! When did you start writing songs?!" I didn't even tell my parents I was doing it—it was just something I would do before I'd go to bed. Now my sister's writing and we're writing together—we actually wrote two songs on the plane together. I don't know . . . she's got a pretty good little writer inside of her.

On the plane, I was sleeping and I woke up and I had this idea in my head for a song and I was looking for paper and so I grabbed—I can't believe I'm gonna say this!—I grabbed the barf bag out of the little folder and I ripped it open and I wrote with a Sharpie because the inside is white. We filled the front and the back with two songs.

Matthew: *What things inspire your songs?*
Haylie: Number one—the problems in our world. I have two songs that are about that, but at the same time they're not slow, dramatic songs. They're about making a difference. And boys always inspire you so there are some songs about them, too!

Matthew: *"Our Lips Are Sealed" became a big hit for you and Hil.*
Haylie: My sister and I grew up loving that song! I think it's a song that everybody knows and loves.

Matthew: *Where do you see yourself going in music?*
Haylie: I'm working on a record deal now. We're meeting with a bunch of different people and talking to a bunch of different labels and whenever we make the album it's gonna be a lot of rock stuff and also a lot of acoustic-sounding stuff as well because those two sides are inside me. I like rock but I also like the Sheryl Crow–type feel as well, and old-school Jewel. My sound is more dance than Hilary's.

Matthew: *Tell me about your movie work.*
Haylie: I had a really, really great experience on *Napoleon Dynamite*. Everyone got along really well. We were in this tiny town in Idaho called Preston, population fifty—they'll hate me for saying that . . . population five hundred! We had a lot of fun there. We would drive every weekend to this lake called Bear Lake, and no joke—it had an overflow of calcium and sulfur or something. It didn't smell or taste weird but it was *turquoise*— the lightest blue in the sky all the way down to the bottom.

I play a mean, snotty girl. I'm the most popular girl in school and I run for class president. At the same time, the three nerds of the school decide they're gonna take over the school by run-

ning as well, so it's this war between the popular kids and the nerdy kids.

Matthew: *Didn't you go to Sundance with* Napoleon Dynamite?

Haylie: I had the best time! I went with one of my best friends. We went to all the screenings and supported the film. Everyone is walking around in Uggs and baseball caps and rolled-up jeans and goes to all the film parties. You meet so many great people.

Matthew: *You're becoming the indie queen, eh?*

Haylie: I also shot *I Love Your Work,* which stars Giovanni Ribisi, and my favorite movie ever is *The Other Sister*—when I got on set and saw him I was so nervous. I was intimidated by how unbelievably talented he is. The movie is about these two celebrities who are like J.Lo and Ben and how a celebrity's life is always intruded on. People keep coming up to him and saying, "I love your work!"

Matthew: *How alike and how different are you and Hilary?*

Haylie: We're a lot alike and then very different at the same time. My sister is very rough-and-tumble, whereas I'm more calm. But then we go shopping together all the time and one of the things we love about that is she'll say, "Look what I got for us!" because we can share clothes.

Matthew: *What would be your ideal movie role?*

Haylie: I haven't read it yet—but I'd want it to be someone young girls can look up to! Everyone thinks to have a teen movie, you have to have somebody take their shirt off or have cussing all the time. I just think the words can be smarter.

Matthew: *You've toured with Hilary. What's been a highlight of that?*

Haylie: Just having this experience and sharing it with my sister is the most special thing.

Matthew: *The tabloids seem to write more about teen stars now than adult stars. Isn't that weird?*

Haylie: Because they're the crazy ones! [Laughs] My sister and I find it kind of embarrassing to be the center of attention, but we can handle it. I'm proud of anything I do that's true. If it's not true, I don't read it!

Heaven . . . or Even L.A.: Hilary Hits the Road and Hits the Big-time!

Almost defiantly in light of their past problems in the City of Angels, Hilary, Haylie, and Susan took up what would become permanent residence in Los Angeles. Bob had witnessed his daughters' determination and had to respect it, so he and his wife decided the best thing for all their futures would be for him to maintain the family homes in Texas and visit Los Angeles at least once a month. It was a sacrifice, but one Hilary and Haylie's parents felt was a wise investment in their girls' futures.

Hilary is very aware of the sacrifices her mom has made to help get her and Haylie where they are today . . . and it sometimes leads to pangs of guilt when she momentarily forgets! She once told *Popstar!* that her guiltiest moment ever was when she talked back to her mom.

" Hilary "

"I did it the other day before my performance because I wanted my hair straight and she didn't and then I felt really bad afterward because she does so much for me—she sacrifices so much and works so hard. I feel so bad that I did it. So I said, 'I'm never gonna do it again!' I felt *sooo* guilty!"

Settling in Los Angeles, Hilary was plunged into the world of moviemaking, but was perhaps fortunate to have a straight-to-video film as her first major part—the pressure on such a set was far less than it would have been on the set of a major motion picture. Director Sean Patrick McNamara had cast Hilary as Wendy for her bubbly quality and found her to be a natural, a born star.

Not that even naturally gifted actresses can't make mistakes. One of Hilary's most embarrassing professional moments came early in her career!

"On the set of my first movie, *Casper Meets Wendy,* I was chasing a goat for this one scene," she told *Girls' Life* magazine. "The director kept screaming, 'Meaner! Meaner!' I ran faster with this really angry expression on my face. But it turned out the goat's *name* was Meaner!"

Oops.

That one goof aside, the video wrapped on time and on budget and Susan knew immediately that while it may not have been a prestigious kind of release, it was a charming family flick and an outstanding calling card. For future castings, she could simply hand over a video with her daughter excelling in a leading role for an hour and a half.

More auditions followed and connections were made. People couldn't help but fall in love with Hilary and Haylie. Karen Bradford recalls of the Duffs, "I think I met Hilary and her sister, Haylie, when Hilary was nine years old. Like most aspiring actors who want to make it in Hollywood, they came to try their luck and just dreamed of getting a part on a show.

"Hilary always had that dazzling smile, was a fun kid and the type of child you wanted your kid around. She would have the best time playing hide-and-seek with Kevin, my son, and never seemed to have a malicious bone in her body."

One of Hilary's and Haylie's early jobs together was in a pilot called *Underworld.* The sci-fi project is one that was so bad—and that was filmed when she was so young—Hilary can't even remember it! During a 2004 *Rolling Stone* interview, Haylie had to remind Hilary of the pilot by telling her that they played little girls in a car whose windshield was smashed by aliens.

Oh—*that* pilot.

Hilary's next success was a long time coming. She and her sister were only getting work sporadically.

Hilary Duff

"Hil and I were very lucky because we were raised in a family that's very positive," Haylie told me. "My mom is very optimistic about things. When we were younger and we'd want a role really bad and didn't get it, she'd say, 'So what? You have an audition tomorrow and the next day, so what are you even worried about?'"

One of those auditions came for Hilary after her mom read the script for *The Soul Collector*. The work's religious overtones were a bonus for the Duffs, who had started Hilary and Haylie on a Christian-influenced homeschooling program—Hilary never set foot in a public school after the age of ten. She never really missed middle school, though, telling interviewer Bob Jamieson in 2002 that she loved the personal attention that homeschooling affords.

After a tough audition process, Hilary landed the juicy role of Ellie in *The Soul Collector,* a dramatic TV movie. The 1999 telefilm followed the story of an angel sent to live among human beings for a month.

In *The Soul Collector,* Hilary got to work with respected actor Bruce Greenwood and *Little House on the Prairie* veteran Melissa Gilbert, who just a few years later would become the president of the Screen Actors Guild. She couldn't have known it at the time, but Melissa's past as a child star was actually a parallel to Hilary's future as one. Hilary remembers the production fondly and this movie has gained a large cult following over the years despite being unavailable on DVD.

Hilary was outstanding in *The Soul Collector.* Susan was bursting with pride, and yet she was pleasantly surprised when Hilary was nominated for a Young Artist Award for Best Performance in a TV Movie or Pilot (Supporting Young Actress). The Duffs attended the ceremony and were blown away when, years into their journey toward establishing Hilary as a working actress, Hilary Duff actually *won* the award!

Maybe this is one reason why, when asked to name the best thing that ever happened to her, Hilary said firmly, "Coming to California was a good thing!"

There is no indication that at any point Hilary seriously missed Texas. She's one of those people who hits Los Angeles and falls in love with its idyllic sunshine, bustling shops, and devotion to the entertainment biz. All she would say later when asked about her home state was that she missed "good Mexican food, the Galleria [mall], and people being so nice!"

For Susan's part, she was realizing it was a "twisted business" she was

helping her daughters navigate. Casting directors were sometimes quite callous about her children's feelings and the competitive atmosphere could be suffocating. She went to great lengths to shield Hilary and Haylie from the brunt of the rejection.

"I will do anything possible to protect her," she told *Blender* magazine as part of a cover story on Hilary in 2004.

As time dragged on with no more juicy roles, one thing Susan did to make herself feel better about Hilary's state of mind was to sit her down and tell her to follow her dreams, but that if she ever wanted to drop out of the business and go home to Texas, Susan would support that decision. It was incredibly liberating and comforting for Hilary.

Susan was there for Hilary when her daughter had to get glasses for impaired vision (one eye is weaker than the other, though she can do without the glasses) and she was there for all of the little setbacks that come with the territory.

It wasn't all gloom and doom in Hollywood. Hilary managed to get a very small part in a film called *Dancing About Architecture.* This was a step in the right direction for Hilary because it would mean time on a real movie set. What's more, the film would star an array of celebrated actors, including Sean Connery, Angelina Jolie, and Ryan Phillippe.

As exciting as the opportunity was, there was a lesson to be learned. The film, despite being intended as a major release for Miramax and having a slew of big names, was delayed over and over. It was eventually renamed *Playing by Heart,* and finally came out at the end of 1998.

Hilary also won a bigger part in a quirky film called *Human Nature.* Again, Hilary was blessed to be in good company. She would play the young Lila Jute, a character played as an adult by Patricia Arquette. In this critically acclaimed film, Hilary's character has a bizarre problem with body hair and has a very emotional scene. Hilary had never done anything like that, but she did it perfectly and the end result, while earning its R rating, is a mesmerizing, disturbing flick, one that would be released in 2001.

In 2000, upon completing *Human Nature,* twelve-year-old Hilary got what should have become her big break. After trying out for countless pilots, she was finally cast in one!

Hilary was chosen to portray one of the daughters of a stay-at-home dad played by Michael Chiklis, who had already become a famous actor thanks to his Emmy-worthy role in *The Commish.* In this sitcom, Hilary would be given good screen time and could expect a shot at becoming part of a long-running, lucrative series.

Hilary was ecstatic. All her dreams were coming true. The Duffs allowed their hopes to escalate to new heights as they awaited word on when the pilot would be shot. NBC, the network behind *Daddio*, was at the peak of its power with shows like *Friends* and *Frasier* revving up its schedule. Would Hilary become a part of "Must-See TV"?

Nope.

When *Daddio* bowed on March 23, 2000, it was without Hilary Duff. The producers had reassessed their choice of Hilary and decided that she was not right for the part after all. She was replaced by Cristina Kernan, an effervescent girl who had wanted to be a model but whose petite size led her to try acting instead. Amazingly, she had been chosen to bump Hilary, who had struggled to win roles for years in Hollywood, only *three weeks* after her first professional audition!

As impossible as it may seem to believe, replacing actors—even impressionable youngsters—is very common at that stage of the game with pilots. In fact, many actors are replaced after a pilot has been shot and aired, and sometimes even after a few episodes have been televised. What might seem inexcusable to those of us on the outside looking in is actually commonplace in Tinseltown. Susan Duff knew this. Hilary did not.

Hilary wanted to give up. She even asked, albeit not too forcefully, to go back to Texas. Susan recognized a momentary depression in her daughter—one that was perfectly understandable given the harsh setback they'd just faced. She kept Hilary auditioning, and urged her to keep an appointment to try out for the lead role in a new Disney Channel series to be entitled *What's Lizzie Thinking?*

Hilary was not enthusiastic and almost tried to cancel the audition. Had she done so, you would not be reading this book, because *What's Lizzie Thinking?* would be retitled *Lizzie McGuire* and it would make Hilary Duff a household name!

Quiz

The Ultimate Hilary Trivia Test!

1. What was the name of a song Haylie once wrote for Hilary?
- **A.** "I Need a Sunday"
- **B.** "I'm a Pepper"
- **C.** "Pop Holiday"
- **D.** "Let's Par-Tay"

2. What TV show did Hilary say she'd love to appear on . . . except it would mean she'd only get to wear one outfit all season?
- **A.** *The West Wing*
- **B.** *Phil of the Future*
- **C.** *Summerland*
- **D.** *24*

3. What reality show did Hilary say she'd most likely do well on?
- **A.** *Fear Factor*
- **B.** *The Real World*
- **C.** *The Amazing Race*
- **D.** *The Apprentice*

4. What kind of dog is Hilary's pooch, Macy?
- **A.** Pit bull
- **B.** Border collie
- **C.** Chihuahua
- **D.** Pomeranian

5. What was Lizzie McGuire's middle name?
- **A.** Harriet
- **B.** Andrea
- **C.** Rhonda
- **D.** Brooke

6. Which of the following TV shows has Hilary never appeared on?
- **A.** *Australian Idol*
- **B.** *The O.C.*
- **C.** *TRL*
- **D.** *American Dreams*

7. In what state has Hilary lived at some point in her life?
- **A.** Rhode Island
- **B.** California
- **C.** Louisiana
- **D.** Florida

8. In her "Come Clean" video, what color is Hilary's sweater?
- **A.** White
- **B.** Red
- **C.** Black
- **D.** Green

9. Prefame, Hilary had to overcome a minor problem that might have hurt her at auditions. What was it?
- **A.** A hard time remembering dialogue
- **B.** A speech impediment that made *R*'s hard to say
- **C.** Stage fright
- **D.** Uncontrollable giggling

10. Which of Hilary's projects is set during the Civil War?
- **A.** *Casper Meets Wendy*
- **B.** *The Lizzie McGuire Movie*
- **C.** *True Women*
- **D.** *The Perfect Man*

11. Which of Hilary's *Cheaper by the Dozen* costars gave her driving advice during the filming of the movie?

    A. Bonnie Hunt
    B. Steve Martin
    C. Ashton Kutcher
    D. Tom Welling

12. Name the TV show on which Hilary appeared in segments called "Hilary's Hits" to coach kids on baseball terms.

    A. *Kids on Deck*
    B. *Bleacher Bums*
    C. *Home Run Hilary*
    D. *Joey*

13. Hilary has been called an ambassador for what famous doll line?

    A. Barbie! She and Haylie are promoting Fashion Fever Barbie in an ad campaign!
    B. Bratz! She just loves their attitude and talks them up constantly in interviews!
    C. Holly Hobbie! Hil rocks to the old-school vibe!
    D. Cabbage Patch Kids! Because Hilary's dad invented them!

14. At The 2004 MTV Video Music Awards, with whom did Hilary present the award for Best Rap Video?

    A. Orlando Bloom
    B. Jeremy Sumpter
    C. Matthew Lillard
    D. Haylie Duff

15. What was the first single released from Hilary's self-titled album?

    A. "Someone's Watching Over Me"
    B. "Why Not"
    C. "Fly"
    D. "Little Voice"

16. Hilary won an award as "Today's Superstar" at which ceremony?

    A. The 2004 Movieline Young Hollywood Awards
    B. The 2003 Grammys
    C. The 1999 Miss Rising Star Contest
    D. The 1998 Casper Awards

17. Who plays Hilary's mother in *The Perfect Man*?

    A. Madonna
    B. Hallie Todd
    C. Britney Spears
    D. Heather Locklear

18. What's the name of the clothing line for pets created by Hilary?

    A. Little Dog Duff Stuff
    B. Ruff-Ruff Stuff
    C. Dressed to the K-Nines
    D. Bow Wow Wow!

19. In *Cheaper by the Dozen*, what did the sign spell out when the whole family held up letters on the football field?

    A. WE SUPPORT OUR DAD
    B. WE LOVE THE COACH
    C. JUST KIDDING AROUND
    D. DADS RULE

20. With what famous actor did Hilary appear at E! Online's Sizzlin' 16 Party in January of 2002?

    A. Jordy Masterson
    B. Frankie Muniz
    C. Aaron Carter
    D. Chad Michael Murray

20-B	16-A	12-A	8-A	4-D
19-B	15-C	11-D	7-B	3-A
18-A	14-C	10-C	6-B	2-D
17-D	13-A	9-B	5-D	1-A

Answers

Where Did I Go Right? The Complete *Lizzie McGuire* Story!

After *Lizzie McGuire* had already made her famous, Hilary joked to the *National Enquirer* that being fired from *Daddio* was "lucky." She wasn't kidding around! If Hilary had been tied down to *Daddio*, she would not have been able to audition for *Lizzie McGuire*, even though *Daddio* was canceled and aired its tenth and last episode in October of 2000.

Hilary found the audition process for what was then called *What's Lizzie Thinking?* to be quite rigorous, but that's to be expected considering she was trying out for the lead in a series. She was called back several times over the course of two weeks. Having already bottomed out over *Daddio*, Hilary did not hold out much hope for her future with Disney Channel—if it was gonna happen, it was gonna happen.

What made *What's Lizzie Thinking?* even more special was that Disney Channel was taking some creative chances with it. The network announced in an unusually effusive press release that the series would make use of "16mm film, high-8 video, digital stills and animation." The animation would be used to bring to life a character known as Animated Lizzie. This cartoon of Lizzie would appear from time to time on-screen to enhance Lizzie's thoughts and to communicate directly to the tween audience.

What Hilary could not have known was just how dazzled the show's creative team was by, well, just by her ability to shine from within!

Now that Hilary is famous, some detractors find her persona to be that of a goody-goody, or even say she is just playing up that side of her personality as a calculated business move. Nothing could be further from the truth.

"Now when I look at Hilary," says Karen Bradford today, "I still see that same sweet girl I first met. Hilary has not changed. I hear people say she's too 'sweetsy-cutesy' and I just think, 'You know her now that she is popular—you never knew her when.'"

Karen is convinced Hilary's fame comes from her naturally positive personality, the same personality that was winning over the producers of *What's Lizzie Thinking?*

Hilary Duff

22

"I think Hilary is a success because when she started the show, kids identified with her sweetness. It was a refreshing breeze!"

Finally, Hilary was informed that the quest for Lizzie had been narrowed down to three girls, including herself. At that point, she realized she was very close to having her own TV show—and she was only twelve!

"I was so scared!" she recalled in *Popstar!* magazine. But there was nothing to do but come in for a final callback and be herself. The producers were eager to find a young actress who did not have to stretch to come across as a likable, normal girl, someone other girls would at once look up to and relate to as a peer.

At last, Hilary was told: You're it! She was tagged to play Elizabeth Brooke "Lizzie" McGuire! She was offered a starting salary of $15,000 per episode, a fee that would increase to $35,000 per episode by the time the series ended.

What's Lizzie Thinking? began production in Los Angeles in August of 2000. As of September 1, Disney Channel had ordered twenty episodes, all of which were filmed in a relatively short period of time, and the show was rechristened *Lizzie McGuire*—a wise way of getting viewers to focus on the star of the show, and of creating a brand.

Hilary had been forced to adapt to long periods of inactivity when she first arrived in L.A.; now she was being asked to work every day for hours at a time.

"Working every day is a big adjustment," she later observed. But as she candidly told *Teen Vogue*, "Working is what makes me really happy."

She *did* have to spend a certain amount of her day being schooled on the set, but thanks to Susan's homeschooling, Hilary was used to this kind of arrangement and it didn't faze her.

"I have a tutor that goes everywhere with me on set. I only have to do it for two and a half hours a day."

Making the transition easier was the fact that a friend of Hilary's, Lalaine Vergara-Paras, was cast to play her best friend, Miranda. Hilary and Lalaine were only living a block apart and had attended dance classes together. They'd seen each other around at auditions. They started the series as friends and would share many fun times over the next two years.

Hilary bonded right away with Adam Lamberg, the older guy (by three years) who had been signed to play Gordo.

"She's the greatest," Adam told me. "I . . . sort of learned how to be her

friend but not get involved in the girly stuff."

Hilary recalls having to jump on Adam to wake him up when it was his turn to be in a scene.

She loved the entire cast and crew, and received great advice from her on-screen parents, Hallie Todd and Robert Carradine, who is a member of the famous Carradine acting family.

Hilary found that all of her script reading and years of auditioning had conditioned her for the heavy memorization required of a girl who was in practically every scene of her own show. She quickly fell into a rhythm and soon was able to take in whole pages with little more than a glance.

"I think we're totally alike in our clothes, makeup, and hair. I think she's a little more insecure," Hilary told a reporter, about Lizzie, when the show was in its early days.

Producer Stan Rogow knew that Hilary, and the other cast members, were creating their roles as much as the writers were.

"She certainly knows more about being a thirteen-year-old today than any of us," he said in a press release, "and that's an example of how each and every one of these cast members is doing a version of themselves and bringing so much to his or her role."

Disney Channel was very pleased with the finished episodes, though they would wind up airing them out of order to lead off with the one they felt was the strongest, called "Rumors."

Rumors of the show's potential were hard to keep down. Disney Channel itself trumpeted the series as "a trailblazing take on a tween's antics and emotions."

Observers didn't have to take their word for it. In the January 16, 2001, issue of *Variety*, Laura Fries wrote, "*Lizzie McGuire*, formerly called *What's Lizzie Thinking?*, is a clever and whimsical show that explores the inner child of, well, a child."

On Sunday, January 19, 2001, at 6:00 P.M. EST, "Rumors" aired on Disney Channel, kicking off what would become the network's number one series and one of its greatest pop cultural legacies.

The ratings of *Lizzie McGuire* were, as *Variety* might say, boffo! For starters, it was the highest-rated debut of any Disney Channel series among kids and tweens of all ages. And it only improved over time. By February 9, Disney had ordered more episodes.

Hilary wasn't as enthusiastic as the critics at seeing herself on the small screen! She initially hated seeing how she looked and acted and was her own harshest critic. She gave up watching the episodes when they aired, but often watched the unfinished producer's cut to make sure she was performing up to her ability.

There was another, almost immediate side effect that Hilary was not prepared for at first. As Karen Bradford points out, "She probably never imagined that she would achieve superstardom."

Early in the show's run, Hilary became recognizable among her age group, well before parents and other adults had ever heard of her.

She told the *National Enquirer* of the first of many fan encounters: "These punked-out girls wearing leather jackets and spiked clothes with bright red hair came up to me and I was thinking, 'Wow, I'm gonna get beat up.' But they smiled the biggest smile and said, 'We're fans, can we have your autograph?'"

While it made Hilary happy to know that people liked the show, she was taken aback by the level of enthusiasm.

"I was doing this thing in California where they wanted me to sit in this really cool car and wave to neighbors and stuff," she explained of another wild encounter "I was doing it and then this one girl flips out—she was probably seventeen. She started screaming at the top of her lungs and running. She was scream-ing, 'Oh, my God! Hilary!' She was running and pushing all of these people out of her way. She trips and fell on the concrete, rips up her jeans, gets up, and starts running toward the car again. She grabs me and she's trying to pull me out of the car. It was so scary!"

She also got countless phone calls in 2001 at home, always won-dering, *How did they get my number?*

Fans developed an insatiable appetite for information about their fave new star. "I think one of them asked me what kind of toothpaste I use and one asked me how I get my bangs like I do."

As the first season was filmed, Hilary wound up having a fan moment of her own—when Aaron Carter was signed to guest star playing himself! She'd met him at his birthday party and sparks had flown. They had great chemistry and Aaron knew how to make a girl feel special. Filming his spot for the show, they became an item.

"Meeting Aaron was really fun," she told MSN in an on-line chat, "and it was fun working with him." But she was less excited about their on-screen smooch! "The kiss was embarrassing because there were like two hundred people around and that was embarrassing . . . but it was fun!" Aaron later recalled having to shoot the kiss "about thirty times."

When "Aaron Carter Is Coming to Town" premiered on March 23, 2001, some fans were titillated by Hilary and Aaron's on-screen lovey-dovey behavior, and others were flat-out angry. Hilary learned a valuable lesson about keeping her dates private so as not to upset her fans or those of a famous boyfriend. Many of Aaron's fans lashed out on message boards about Hilary "stealing" their heartthrob, in the same way so many had been angry toward Britney Spears when they found out that she was dating Justin Timberlake.

Hilary's schedule today is famously crowded. When *Lizzie* took off, she began to experience the first problems associated with being stretched too thin. As ecstatic as the Duffs were for Hilary's success, it was not without its drawbacks.

"My friends who aren't actors, if I'm really busy and I told them the day before, 'Oh, I don't think I'm going to be busy so we can hang out,' or something like that, they don't get it if I can't hang out," Hilary once told me. "You have to really sacrifice a lot—give up going to hang out with your friends one night to go to the studio and record." Still, Hilary has never regretted her showbiz decisions. "I love it, so it's not like I'm going to regret it when I'm older. But it's really hard."

Besides her shooting schedule, Hilary was required to promote the show in a variety of ways, from filming assorted segments for Disney Channel to appearing at The 19th Annual Walt Disney World Christmas Day Parade. The show's popularity was quickly expanded upon in a myriad of ways, including a popular minisite at ZoogDisney.com that raked in 200,000 fan e-mails a week.

By July of 2001, twenty-two more episodes of *Lizzie* had been ordered and Hilary had begun to attract the attention of magazines popular with young girls.

As I described in my introduction to this book, *Popstar!*'s first contact with Hilary was a Disney's California Adventure two-day trip with Kyla Pratt and Shia LaBeouf. Photographer Chris Garlington remembers this assignment as "one of my favorite shoots. Hilary was a blast to work with. She has a great personality and the camera *loves* her."

Though this was Hilary's first major exposure to the teen press, she was anything but shy and retiring!

Chris recalls, "One of the funniest moments from our two days together was when we ate lunch at the ABC Soap Opera Bistro. One of the chefs was named Elizabeth McGuire. She took out her Disney ID card and, sure enough, the McGuire girls posed for a photo! We all got quite a laugh out of it."

The kids went from ride to ride at the theme park, and Chris remembers Shia starting a water fight that Kyla and Hilary finished. "Hilary was running around the park barefoot and soaked, trying to get Shia back! They made quite a scene and it made for some great photos!"

When the layout appeared in the August 2001 issue of *Popstar!*, it was Hilary's first major coverage in the media, and it came with her first-ever full-page pinup.

After the September 11th attacks on America, Hilary and a lineup of other stars filmed patriotic "Express Yourself" public service announcements that ran on Disney Channel. The intended effect was to rally Americans, but it also ratcheted up Hilary's star power. Another factor in Hilary's escalating fame was when *Lizzie McGuire* began airing Saturday mornings on ABC that fall.

Accolades poured in. *Lizzie McGuire*'s first season won for Favorite Television Series at Nickelodeon's 15th Annual Kids' Choice Awards. Hilary was nominated in the acting category but lost out to Amanda Bynes, a Nickelodeon star. In January of 2002 and 2003, Hilary was chosen as one of E! Online's Sizzlin' 16 Young Hollywood Stars.

"It's really cool, because I've worked really hard to get to where I am right now," she said at the time, though most of her fans assumed she was an overnight sensation. "It's a little strange, but it's cool in a way, too." Hilary appeared at a charity benefit for the Disney Adventures All-Star Program, drawing hundreds of fans.

Two personally enriching opportunities arose out of *Lizzie McGuire*'s success—first, Hilary was asked to record music to capitalize on her fame. By 2002, she had recorded the infectious pop song "I Can't Wait" for an official *Lizzie McGuire Soundtrack*, and the video was hugely successful on Disney Channel and all the major kid-vid outlets. The other was that movie offers came Hilary's way, including one for a feature film based on *Lizzie McGuire* that was going to be set in Rome.

Hilary earned her first-ever magazine cover in April 2002, when she graced *Popstar!* in character as Lizzie McGuire. Inside, she lamented her boy troubles ("They'll stand there, but they are too embarrassed to come up and say something!"), and dished behind-the-scenes details about the show. It was the magazine's best-selling issue of the year, thanks in part to being timed to coincide with the airing of Hilary's first movie for Disney Channel.

Disney Channel, enamored of their new star, had signed Hilary up for an original movie called *Cadet Kelly*, a teen take on Goldie Hawn's acclaimed comic romp *Private Benjamin. Cadet Kelly* began filming July 30, 2001. In the film, Hilary's character, Kelly Collins, is yanked from a New York City private school and sent to a military academy, where she competes with a talented nemesis played by the *Even Stevens* actress (and now recording star) Christy Carlson Romano.

"Being mean to Hilary was challenging because she's so sweet," Christy has admitted.

For this role, Hilary withstood two weeks of cadet training to go through the same hard work Kelly had to go through. She also "read the script like a million times" to find ways in which to make Kelly different from Lizzie.

"I felt like Kelly was this really cool girl who was such a free spirit and had so much energy," she said. In some ways, Kelly was even more like Hilary than Lizzie herself!

A Lizzie-esque moment for Hilary occurred early in the filming.

"I'm in the middle of doing this scene where I'm practicing to try out for the corps. In the middle of doing a take, I throw the gun up in the air. All of the extras in the movie had already been through the school, so they all knew how to do this stuff really well and I throw it up and it comes down and it clunks me on the head!"

Still, Hilary loved the physical aspect of the role. "Going through military training for a whole month, tossing and spinning rifles, and learning how to do the exchanges [of the rifles] with other people . . . it actually got kind of addictive, because I didn't want to stop!"

The hardest part of filming was one of the final scenes.

"The very last day of filming was when we did Kelly in boot camp training when Jennifer's being really mean and makes her stay on the course until late in the evening," Hilary said. "When we did that scene, it was so cold and it was three o'clock in the morning. They were spraying the fake rain and it turned the dirt into mud." In Toronto, the mud is more like wet clay, so Hilary was caked with the stuff. "I must have had ten cups of hot chocolate that night!"

Hilary's favorite scene in *Cadet Kelly* was the part where she dangles from the side of a cliff. "I really liked getting to do my own stunts!"

Cadet Kelly debuted on March 8, 2002. It was a blockbuster for Disney Channel, reeling in 7.8 million viewers and leading to record ratings for *Lizzie McGuire*, as well.

Despite her anything-but-average life, Hilary was concerned about normal teen things . . . like learning to drive! She claimed she had done a good job practicing during the holidays in 2002 with her dad's help. But she had more trouble "when I'm in the car with my mom because she is like, 'Stop! Stop! Stop!'"

There was no stopping her career. After years of struggling, Hilary Duff's status as a rising star was cruising at 90 M.P.H.

"It's all a big blur," she said in her *Popstar!* cover story. "Even though it didn't happen fast—it happened in four years—it's kind of weird."

She had filmed the final episodes of *Lizzie McGuire* (Disney Channel normally only shoots a sixty-five-episode run) by June of 2002, leaving Hilary with a lot of choices. She could pursue a music career, sign up for a *Lizzie* movie (a script called *Ciao, Lizzie!* looked promising), take on other non-Disney films (the March 26, 2002, edition of the *Hollywood Reporter* stated that Hilary was about to be signed by New Line for a flick called *Confessions of a Teenage Drama Queen*), or possibly do a high school version of *Lizzie* for ABC that would run as a series during prime time.

She was offered $1 million to be *Lizzie* on the big screen and could have made $100,000 per episode for the ABC version.

"I like doing TV because it keeps me in Los Angeles with my friends and stuff. I also really love doing movies, but that takes me out of town. It's kind of fifty/fifty and that's what I'm trying to figure out right now," she said. Ultimately, Hilary Duff would accept the offer to shoot the retitled *The Lizzie McGuire Movie*.

On top of *The Lizzie McGuire Movie*, she would also take on other film projects, all the while developing her blossoming musical career.

But she would never again play Lizzie on TV.

After filming the final episode, Hilary flew to Vancouver to film a supporting role in *Agent Cody Banks* opposite Frankie Muniz, leaving her no time to mourn the loss.

Hilary reminisced about the unforgettable TV series in 2004: "I loved working on *Lizzie McGuire*. I worked every day for two years and when you work every day on something, it can get kind of tiring, but I loved the cast and crew . . . they were amazing."

Hilary's life and career at that point could be neatly summed up by a quote Hilary gave to MSN: "If you have a dream, go after it, keep on trying, it will pay off."

"If you have a dream, go after it, keep on trying it will pay off."

Adam Lamberg: Brotherly Love!

What would *Lizzie McGuire* have been without lovable Gordo to play Lizzie's sidekick? Gordo had a wisdom about him (in reality, Adam was born September 14, 1984, making him more than three years *older* than Hilary!) and seemed to love Hilary from afar. He was part of some of the zaniest episodes and even became a huge part of *The Lizzie McGuire Movie*, something even Miranda (Lalaine) didn't achieve.

Adam Matthew Lamberg was born in New York City, which should not surprise fans considering Gordo's decidedly East Coast accent. He began to act when he was just seven years old, but it was only to help out a director in need! Adam's cousin introduced him to a casting director who was looking—desperately— for just the right boy for a TV commercial.

"There was a job for a little kid in his commercial," Adam told me. "He had been auditioning kids for a long time and he hadn't found the right kid. So he was telling everyone he knew, 'If you know a little kid, send them on the audition.'" Adam went in, read, scored the job, and fell head over heels for acting.

Adam has appeared in movies like *I'm Not Rappaport* and in the indie film The *Pirates of Central Park* (with Jesse McCartney), but now that he's taking time out to attend college, he can easily look back and see that *Lizzie McGuire* was his big break.

Adam was so tight with Hilary he flew to Toronto for a major Kids With A Cause benefit in 2003!

Not that playing Gordo was a huge stretch for Adam!

"Gordo and I are kind of similar. Gordo is smart and witty and I hope I'm like that!"

In real life, Adam is just as nice as Gordo—maybe more! Now that Hilary is a big-time star, you might think he'd be into dishing dirt on his former costar. No way!

"I've gotten to know Hilary pretty well. I can have, like, *total* fun with the girl. We're always joking around—not so much playing pranks on each other, though that does happen, too. She listens to music that I can talk to her about, stuff like that. She's amazing."

As for acting, Adam will next be seen in a grown-up movie called *When Do We Eat?* costarring Shiri Appleby.

Quiz
Take the Lizzie McChallenge!

1. On what date did *Lizzie McGuire* first air on Disney Channel?
   A. April 4, 2000
   B. January 19, 2001
   C. December 16, 2002
   D. February 13, 2004

2. Which cute actor plays Lizzie's crush, Ethan Craft?
   A. Clayton Snyder
   B. Chad Michael Murray
   C. Adam Lamberg
   D. Lalaine

3. What contest do Lizzie, Gordo, and Miranda lose in the "Facts of Life" episode?
   A. All-School Super Quiz
   B. Math Olympics
   C. Factathlon
   D. Third Annual Dog Show

4. Name Lizzie's snobby rival.
   A. Kate
   B. Angie
   C. Miranda
   D. Lindsay

5. What school does Lizzie attend?
   A. Hillride Junior High
   B. Los Angeles Middle School
   C. Abraham Lincoln Elementary
   D. Jennifer Lopez School of Dance

6. What is Gordo's real name?
   A. David Joseph George
   B. David Zephyr Gordon
   C. Gordon Reynolds Jr.
   D. Dave Matthews

7. Which famous performer never appeared on Lizzie McGuire?
   A. Aaron Carter
   B. Steve Tyler
   C. Doris Roberts
   D. Barney

8. Who is Lizzie's bratty brother?
   A. Matt
   B. Bill
   C. Sam
   D. Prince Michael Jackson IV

9. Which of these characters flunked kindergarten?
   A. Lizzie
   B. Gordo
   C. Kate
   D. Grandma McGuire

10. What R-rated movie did Lizzie & Co. sneak into?
   A. *Vesuvius*
   B. *Volcano*
   C. *Lava*
   D. *Red-Hot Mountain*

11. What famous actress played Gordo's girlfriend on the episode where Miranda dresses up as a boy?
   A. Kyla Pratt from *Fat Albert*
   B. Brittany Snow from *American Dreams*
   C. Jamie Lynn Spears from *Zoey 101*
   D. Emma Roberts from *Unfabulous*

12. What's the name of the coffee place Lizzie and her friends hang out at?
A. Electric Youth
B. Digital Bean
C. Café de Café
D. The Peach Pit

13. Lizzie got a brief kiss from Aaron Carter, but her first real kiss came from the . . . ?
A. Paperboy
B. Busboy
C. Neighbor boy
D. La-Z-Boy

14. How many episodes of *Lizzie McGuire* were filmed?
A. 600
B. 100
C. 65
D. 3, but they rerun them a *lot*

18. Which Latin singer appeared on the episode called "El Oro de Montezuma"?
A. Marc Anthony
B. Enrique Iglesias
C. Shalim
D. Chingy

15. This bad girl corrupted Lizzie, prompting Gordo to direct a *Before They Were Bad Girls* video.
A. Sally
B. Angel
C. Deb
D. Cruella

19. What school dance convinces Lizzie she and Ethan are not meant to be?
A. Homecoming Dance
B. Junior Prom
C. Sadie Hawkins Dance
D. The Ethan Doesn't Like Lizzie Spring Formal

16. Miranda proved she couldn't act in what school production?
A. *Saturday Night Fever*
B. *Cabaret*
C. *Chicago*
D. *Greasier*

20. In "The Greatest Crush of All," Lizzie and Miranda are competing for the attentions of what forget-about-it older guy?
A. Their handsome teacher
B. A supercute teen-mag coverguy
C. The hottest track coach in history
D. An elderly traffic cop

17. Lizzie once went out on a date with . . . ?
A. Larry Tudgeman
B. Ethan Craft
C. Gordo
D. Matt

Acting Up with Kate: Meet the Real Ashlie Brillault!

"That was a blast being able to do that," says Ashlie Brillault of her years playing Kate Sanders on Disney Channel's *Lizzie McGuire*, "doing something that you *love* to do for a career!"

But some of the biggest *Lizzie McGuire* fans have a hard time accepting that Ashlie Brillaut—so brilliant as nasty Kate Sanders—is really a nice girl!

"It's funny because people come up to me and they're always scared," confesses Ashlie. "I'm just like, 'What? It's just me!' I guess they all see me as Kate, but then after they talk to me they're like, 'Oh, yeah, she's nice.'" But sometimes the scared fans will have their moms make the first contact with Ashlie . . . just in case!

Ashlie gets spotted all the time, thanks to the eternal reruns of *Lizzie McGuire* on Disney Channel. And when fans notice her, she notices them!

"They just keep looking back at you and then they start whispering to their friends. When I see that happening, I'll smile or wave at them," Ashlie says. "This little girl came up to me and was like, 'You know what? You're so mean to Lizzie McGuire—I hate you so much. I want to kick you right now!' I was like, 'Oh, my gosh! Please don't kick me. I'm not like that—I swear!'"

It might make some of Kate's antifans feel better to know that even Ashlie Brillault, a pretty TV star, had problems in school.

"I didn't like middle school *at all* because of how many people were like Kate—especially because I was doing a lot of modeling and acting so a lot of snobby girls didn't like me. It was a pretty miserable experience!"

Ashlie, like her good friend Hilary, is very involved in charitable work. Along with Kids With A Cause, she has volunteered for one organization in particular called Don't Laugh at Me, which tackles the problem of gossip and put-downs in the school environment. Its message is summed up by Ashlie as, "You shouldn't be like Kate! That's not a fun person to be like."

The best kind of person *to* be like is . . . Ashlie herself. At least, I think so! Ashlie describes herself as someone with a lot more to offer than superficial Kate.

"I'm a nice person," Ashlie says. "I'm pretty chill. I love hanging out with my little sisters—I care about them a lot. I just like being with my friends. I'm normal!"

Ashlie is proud of all she accomplished on Lizzie McGuire *and in* The Lizzie McGuire Movie!

Blond Hair Everywhere: Hilary Acts Up and Becomes a Movie Star!

Hilary's experience with feature films predates *Lizzie McGuire*, but her omnipresence on Disney Channel and her huge success with the TV movie *Cadet Kelly* shaped her film career—no question about it.

For Hilary's first post-fame movie, she wisely chose a high-profile supporting role that very much kept her aimed at the same audience that adored her from *Lizzie McGuire*.

Frankie Muniz told *People* magazine that he had met Hilary when they both lived in the Oakwood Apartments in Burbank "when we were like twelve." He said he'd met Hilary by the pool and that she'd playfully asked him to guest-star on *Lizzie McGuire*.

He wound up appearing on the show and their friendship made Hilary a natural choice to play his love interest in the *Spy Kids*–type teen action flick *Agent Cody Banks*.

Though new to this kind of commercial project, Hilary was able to secure a $500,000 fee—and even got her name above the title after Frankie's!

For Hilary, there was no major acting challenge. She was playing Natalie Connors, daughter of a clueless scientist kidnapped by evil agents, and it was her job to be

"the girl" of the picture. But she enjoyed making the movie, especially the pyrotechnic aspect!

"I definitely have to say the best part of the movie was at the end, when everything was getting blown up!" she told a Japanese reporter.

Though Hilary and Frankie had had a tight friendship that seemed to almost verge on dating, by the time filming commenced they were just buddies. That made their on-screen kiss a bit weird for Hilary.

"It was so embarrassing to kiss Frankie!"

This would not be her last screen kiss—or her last embarrassing one!

While in Vancouver, Canada, shooting *Agent Cody Banks*, Hilary was also still mulling over the idea of starring in a New Line feature called *Confessions of a Teenage Drama Queen*. She loved the script so much and seemed so intent on making the movie that she'd discussed it in the press for several months. The plan was to finish *Cody*, take a week off in New York, and then film *Confessions*. However, details of the deal were never nailed down and Hilary became disenchanted. By December of 2002, she was telling an on-line chat audience, "I'm not sure if I'm going to do that movie because I'm not sure if I can find the time. I would really like to because it's a really great script."

In the meantime, Hilary had decided she would for sure be Lizzie on the big screen. It wasn't a hard decision for Hilary, who'd come to love the character.

"Lizzie McGuire is just a normal fifteen-year-old," Hilary said to the press. "I think that's why so many kids get into the show—she's just into clothes and hair and makeup, and she's really not the most popular girl in school. She's trying to find herself, just like everyone else."

The movie called for Lizzie and her classmates (minus Miranda) to take a class trip to Rome, where Lizzie would be mistaken for a glam Italian pop star, also played by Hilary. The sweet subplot followed how Lizzie dealt with being away from her mom and dad for the first time.

"Spending time away from her family makes her realize how much she misses then and needs them." This was a theme Hilary could relate to, as she definitely missed her dad when she couldn't see him for weeks at a time.

Hilary would get to travel to Europe for this job, she would get to sing for the soundtrack, and she would be able to launch her proper film career with a surefire hit.

"*Lizzie* was a great place to begin my career. I loved the character, as it was very 'safe' for me, and doing the movie was a lot of fun," she later told *Billboard* magazine.

Director Jim Fall had been signed to *Ciao, Lizzie!*, which was renamed *The Lizzie McGuire Movie*. He remembers meeting Hilary and Susan for the first time at—of all places—the Starbucks on Wilshire at Twenty-sixth in Santa Monica, California.

"Hilary had come down from Vancouver for the day, where she was shooting *Agent Cody Banks.* She was in town doing her Christmas CD," Jim says. He was charmed by mother and daughter, and though he was not yet aware of the magnitude of the show's reach, he recognized immediately Hilary's "glow that makes you unable to look away from her. She just has that certain quality. She's a classic star, one in a million."

The first scene of *The Lizzie McGuire Movie* was set for October 14, 2002, in Rome. Hilary and her posse flew out early and Jim says that when they scouted locations the night before they shot, a fan recognized Hilary half a world away from her home base. It was then he knew that the movie had the possibility of being a major hit.

Hilary was introduced to and liked her leading man, actor Yani Gellman, who was playing the caddish Paolo. Yani, like his director, had not understood the popularity of *Lizzie McGuire* when he'd first accepted the part.

But he figured it out when "my nieces and nephews were dropping dead" upon hearing with whom he would be starring.

Yani remembered that the original cast was very welcoming to him, and in fact everyone on the production stayed in the same five-star hotel—many of them on the same floor!

"I was in heaven trying on all the clothes!" Hilary exclaimed of her time on the set. Her role called for some outrageous faux haute couture as well as stylish teen duds. One pair of Isabella's boots had over seven thousand rhinestones! She also learned a great deal from filming in Italy, saying, "I was studying Roman history, so it was perfect."

Hilary, a big eater despite her petite frame, told the press she ate pizza twice daily and was particularly fond of Italian ice cream. "I think I ate gelato every day. It would take me thirty minutes to decide what kind I wanted because there were a hundred flavors!"

As the five-week shoot progressed, Jim Fall continued to be impressed by his star.

"She was a complete professional," Jim says today. "The series was wrapped and she was so used to the role it was easy to get things in one or two takes. I would have liked more time with her to get even more subtleties out of her performance, but there was no need when she was able to do exactly what was expected so quickly and so naturally."

Jim was especially pleased with the play of emotions on Hilary's face in the scene where she's being told Paolo is not all he seems.

Yani was equally bowled over by Hilary Duff, telling *Popstar!,* "She's a really talented actress. She's really spontaneous and she really acts in the moment, so she keeps every scene really new and fresh and alive. You just go with that, you feed off of it and kind of react to what she brings to the scenes. She brings so much energy and spontaneity and life to the things she does that it really makes your job a lot easier because the chemistry was just there!"

There was not a whole lot of downtime, but what time there was, Hilary seized and maximized!

"It was amazing going over there. I had never been to Europe before so it was cool!" She was able to take side jaunts to Paris and London. She adored London even though she only got to go there for two days for a Disney-sponsored awards show (the *Lizzie McGuire* series won), because she loved the shopping. She also liked Paris, but was uncomfortable, as she was in Italy, with the language barrier.

She racked up 1,500 minutes on her cell phone, earning a reprimand from her dad. It's not good to roam in Rome!

"My favorite thing was getting to see everyone again that we worked with on the show."

Shooting in Rome and Toronto wrapped after Hilary filmed her big performance scenes, and everyone headed home.

When *Agent Cody Banks* was released, it was a sizable hit. It would go on to gross nearly $50 million.

The Lizzie McGuire movie opened soon after (the films were originally scheduled to open within days of each other) and grossed over $17 million in its opening week. Hilary's name was becoming synonymous with Young Hollywood. To many people, Hilary Duff had seemed to come from nowhere to take the crown as the "It" girl of the moment.

"It's interesting how when someone becomes a star, people don't realize that they've been auditioning for the longest while, enduring the disappointments," Karen Bradford of HowToBeAStar.com points out. "When Hilary was at her *The Lizzie McGuire Movie* premiere and she looked like a princess, her mom just looked at me and said, 'Karen, it took six years to be an overnight success.'"

The Lizzie McGuire Movie grossed over $40 million. Disney, of course, wanted a sequel, but there was a problem—Disney wanted another *Lizzie* more than Hilary did. While Hilary would have been happy to do a sequel, Disney didn't pursue her for it until they were sure the first film would be a smash. By then, Hilary had many other projects lined up, among them a romantic comedy called *A Cinderella Story*, pitched as "*Cinderella* meets *Clueless*."

In the end, they decided not to do the *Lizzie McGuire* sequel.

Hilary made a savvy decision not to rush her film career when she accepted a very small supporting role as Lorraine Baker, the second-oldest daughter in a family of twelve kids in *Cheaper by the Dozen*. This family-oriented release from Christmas of 2003 followed the misadventures of a small-town coach (Steve Martin) who relocates to a big city. He's haplessly trying to take full control of his huge family while his wife (Bonnie Hunt) goes on a book tour.

Hilary enjoyed the fun, funny people she met doing this movie, among them Tom Welling and Piper Perabo. For a light work schedule, she was able to be in a heartwarming, quality film that wound up being a monster hit at the box office.

Hilary's next project would not be decided by easy money, and it would not be an artistic cakewalk.

"I want to do everything," she told a writer, "but I think that maybe something I do next I want to be a little more serious because I don't want people to only think that I can only do something funny and, you know, happy like *Lizzie McGuire*."

She decided to sign on for *A Cinderella Story*, directed by Mark Rosman. In it, she'd play Sam, an overworked girl whose father's death has placed her at the mercy of a truly wicked stepmother.

A Cinderella Story allowed Hilary to play a dramatically complex role within a light, fan-pleasing film. She loved that her character underwent a "metamorphosis." This word would get tossed around a lot during the making of *A Cinderella Story* in Los Angeles, and it would become the title of her first major album later on.

The cast and crew of *A Cinderella Story* was top-notch. Susan, Hilary's mom, got an executive producer credit and charming actor Dan Byrd, who became a good pal of Hilary's in real life during the filming, was set to play her male best bud. Since most kids in the business don't attend regular school and miss out on prom, Hilary and Dan hosted a sort of "prom" of their own at his house. Hilary and her friends went to vintage clothing stores and found clothes to wear—her dress was a sequined knockout!

Of course, the most interesting *Cinderella Story* casting choice was heartthrob Chad Michael Murray (of *Freaky Friday* fame), who was signed to play Hilary's love interest.

Hilary and Chad hit it off right away.

"He's really cool! He's so down-to-earth and so nice and a really cool guy!" she would say of her costar. Chad became a welcome part of Hilary's family and he had her accompany him to an event for The WB, the network for which he'd done some pilots and recurring roles and on which he would star in *One Tree Hill*. This, of course, set off alarms in the press, and it was assumed she and Chad were a romantic item. Except . . . they weren't! Not even close. Hilary laughed off the rumors. After all, she had much more vicious rumors to deal with.

Ever since they both dated Aaron Carter, Hilary and Lindsay Lohan have been pitted against each other in the press. This has been a drain on both parties and has created a field day for tabloids unconcerned about printing the truth. To her credit, Hilary has rarely commented on the so-called feud.

Hilary ignored any bad press and enjoyed the long stretch of time at home afforded her by the Los Angeles–based shoot for *A Cinderella Story*. She, her mom, and her sister had since moved into their own house in Toluca Lake, and Hilary was able to schedule photo shoots, interviews, and business meetings nearby instead of arranging them catch-as-catch-can while filming abroad. She was also moving full steam ahead with her musical and merchandising pursuits.

Hilary was especially happy to be able to drive back and forth to the *Cinderella Story* set with her learner's permit, though she was duped by former costar Ashton Kutcher on an episode of his *Punk'd* series because of her passion for driving. Ashton had a phony instructor pull the wool over Hilary's eyes, leading her to believe that she was in the middle of a carjacking. But Hilary has a good sense of humor and laughed it off when she (thankfully!) learned the truth.

When *A Cinderella Story* was released, it became a big hit among the tween and teen crowd. The subject matter was right up their alley and it starred the most famous guy and girl possible. On top of it all, it was a truly dreamy romantic comedy. Hilary was very pleased with the end result.

"I've seen it twice, actually," she's said, "and it's so cute!" She had been nervous because prior to filming, she didn't relate to Sam—so downtrodden, so unspecial—at all.

Behind-the-Scenes: The Making of *Raise Your Voice!*

Gorgeous Oliver James was Hilary's picture-perfect leading man!

Tickling the ivories in preparation for one of Hilary's big singing scenes!

Hil and Ollie film a tense moment!

All smiles, knowing she's making a
movie close to her heart!

<u>Raise Your Voice</u> was originally entitled
<u>Heart of Summer</u>, as this rare set photo
reveals!

It was quite a serious set!

43

Hilary was now a bona fide movie star making $2 million for each picture. She then made another unusual decision about her next project. Instead of doing a high-profile film, she chose to star in a small film called *Heart of Summer* about a girl who loses her brother and goes to a highly competitive performing arts school far from her small-town home, sort of like an L.A. version of *Fame*. The script had been around for a few years and had started out as an untitled Christian music movie.

It makes sense Hilary would be drawn to this project. Her faith is a large part of her life and it was a perfect way to work music into a film in a way that was natural and that would at the same time further her rock-star ambitions.

By the time the film was made, its title had become *Raise Your Voice* and the subject matter had gone from explicitly Christian to being open to a Christian interpretation. The male lead was Oliver James, the British guy who had been Amanda Bynes's love interest in *What a Girl Wants* a couple of years previously.

Oliver was wowed by Hilary, saying, "Hilary's an amazing, professional young girl and she still manages to have a fun life in the middle of her ridiculously hectic schedule! She never stops!"

For her role as Terri Fletcher, Hilary had some serious vocal training to do. She was expected to sing an operatic segment and do lots of vocal gymnastics, whereas with her albums, she had been singing more naturalistically.

"I can sing," she told *Popstar!* for its January 2005 issue, "but I don't think I have the greatest voice, definitely not an opera voice. I have a coach that helped me. They know how to teach people to sing arias."

In the film, Hilary worked with stars David Keith and Rebecca DeMornay and she and her mother, Susan, formed a special bond with Rita Wilson, who played Hilary's beleaguered mother (and who is married to Tom Hanks). The women were dead set on making *Raise Your Voice* a small movie with a big heart. Rita would later cry when she saw a screening of the finished product and called Susan Duff to tell her so.

The youth cast included *Quintuplets* star Johnny Lewis, Kat Dennings from *Raising Dad*, *Joan of Arcadia*'s Jason Ritter (son of the late John Ritter), and singer Lauren C. Mayhew. The kids were in good hands with director Sean Patrick McNamara, whose experience directing young people includes helming Disney Channel's brilliant *Even Stevens* series and, of course, having directed Hilary in her first movie, *Casper Meets Wendy.*

As Hilary filmed *Raise Your Voice*, she was increasingly aware of the media's scrutiny of every aspect of her life. She was already a major singing star and had launched a line of clothes and accessories. She was everywhere, and so were the media!

"I hate them!" she said to *Teen Vogue* of the paparazzi who to this day stalk her wherever she goes. "They follow you! I've had nine cars on me for six hours, no joke."

She also feels strongly that there is a negative side effect of constant criticism, and not only for the celebrities themselves.

"It's sick when the tabloids are criticizing people for what they wear, saying that they're not skinny enough. Everyone feels so much pressure to look a certain way."

She had come to realize that blanket coverage of her personal life, and her appearance, was "the worst part of the job!"

Another side effect of so much media attention is more positive—it helps to put Hilary Duff's name at the top of everyone's list when it comes to casting major movies. She has been connected to many projects and basically has her pick.

Raise Your Voice barely caused a ripple at the multiplex, but all of Hilary's other movies have been not only profitable (as *Raise Your Voice* will be with DVD and other revenues) but phenomenally successful. Her upcoming films seem to be on track to keep Hilary Inc. in the black.

First up, Hilary will appear in *The Perfect Man*, a quirky comedy about a girl named Holly Hamilton who helps to find the right man for her lonely divorcée mom (played by Heather Locklear).

After that, Hilary is committed to *Material Girls*, an outrageous comedy that sends up the Hilton sisters ("You didn't get that from *me!*" Hilary says of the Hilton connection!). Haylie will star alongside Hil in this highly anticipated farce from Madonna's Maverick Films.

Then, Hilary may do a film called *Outward Blonde* that might remind fans of a more grown-up *Cadet Kelly*; Hilary would play a snobby New York princess who flunks PE and is forced to take part in an Outward Bound program.

There is no end in sight for Hilary's film career, but while she has built it up over the past few years, she has worked equally hard in several other areas—and the Hilary story would not be complete with telling those stories as well!

Quiz

Movie Madness!

As Hilary's fan, you should know her films backward and forward by now—but this quiz will challenge even her most diehard devotees! If you get all ten right, you must be . . . Hilary Duff herself!

1. Where was Terri Fletcher from in *Raise Your Voice*?

    A. New York, New York
    B. Los Angeles, California
    C. Santa Fe, New Mexico
    D. Flagstaff, Arizona

2. At the end of *The Lizzie McGuire Movie,* which two characters perform "What Dreams Are Made Of" as a duet?

    A. Paolo and Isabella
    B. Isabella and Lizzie
    C. Lizzie and Gordo
    D. Miranda and Kate

3. "Save the world. Get the girl. Pass math." Which Hilary movie did this phrase help promote?

    A. *Human Nature*
    B. *A Cinderella Story*
    C. *The Lizzie McGuire Movie*
    D. *Agent Cody Banks*

4. "Don't let the fear of striking out keep you from playing the game." Who says this and in which Hilary movie?

    A. Sam's dad in *A Cinderella Story*
    B. Fiona in *A Cinderella Story*
    C. Ms. Ungermeyer in *The Lizzie McGuire Movie*
    D. Jay in *Raise Your Voice*

5. Which character in *The Lizzie McGuire Movie* confesses that girls who don't seem to know everything are "hot"?

   A. Ethan
   B. Gordo
   C. Paolo
   D. Ms. Ungermeyer

6. In *A Cinderella Story,* Mrs. Wells criticizes one student's shirt and then nervously says hi to another student—which guy gets the shy hi?

   A. Ryan (J. D. Pardo)
   B. Carter (Dan Byrd)
   C. Austin (Chad Michael Murray)
   D. David (Brad Bufanda)

7. Where is Miranda in *The Lizzie McGuire Movie*?

   A. Rome, Italy
   B. Mexico City, Mexico
   C. San Diego, California
   D. Flushing, Missouri

8. Which of the following guys was never one of Hilary's leading men?

   A. Yani Gellman
   B. Chad Michael Murray
   C. Lil' Romeo
   D. Frankie Muniz

9. In which movie did a former member of the girl group PYT star alongside Hilary?

    A. Lydia Bell, in *A Cinderella Story*
    B. Tracy Williams, in *Cheaper by the Dozen*
    C. Lauren C. Mayhew, in *Raise Your Voice*
    D. Ashley Niven, in *Playing by Heart*

10. In which of the following did we see Hilary as a brunette?

    A. *Raise Your Voice*
    B. *The Lizzie McGuire Movie*
    C. *A Cinderella Story*
    D. *Human Nature*

Answers

1-D
2-B
3-D
4-A
5-A
6-A
7-B
8-C
9-C
10-B

Girl Can Rock: How Hilary Raised Her Voice to Become a Singing Star!

Hilary Duff's musical career is nothing short of miraculous, when you consider two potential problems she had to overcome in order to pull it off. First, Hilary is not a born singer—since childhood she was much more focused on acting and had only ever sung in classes back in San Antonio. Also, the public often has a hard time accepting actors who suddenly emerge with CDs and demand to be taken seriously as recording artists.

Hilary overcame both possible roadblocks by making the transition slowly and organically.

In 2001, Hilary was making an appearance at a Radio Disney concert in Anaheim, California. She was overwhelmed at the sight of all the pop stars and the fans eagerly awaiting their appearance onstage. She was also already inspired by having met Aaron Carter, whose success in pop had kindled some of Hilary's own ambitions.

Hilary told *Billboard* magazine, "There were all these pop acts backstage at the concert . . . getting ready backstage and warming up, and I was like, 'I want to do this so bad!'"

Hilary was introduced to Andre Recke, who was there as the manager for Myra, a Disney recording act known for sugary pop and an endearing stage presence.

To his credit, Andre immediately sized up Hilary as a potential music superstar, and they began to work together very soon thereafter.

"When I met Hilary, I knew she had something special. Sometimes you just have that feeling, that, 'Wow, she's a star,'" he told *Billboard*.

Soon enough, Hilary was excitedly telling the press, "I'm actually taking singing lessons right now! I sing in the shower, in the car—everywhere!"

In spite of coming to singing later than many professionals, she discovered her range and tested her limits and was able to develop a wonderfully sweet voice, one that is more than capable of hitting all the right notes and—even better—one that sparkles with personality.

One way in which Hilary actually had an advantage in singing as opposed to in acting is that in acting, she started from zero. In singing, she started from the position of being a major children's TV star, one connected to a corporation with many musical outlets—Disney had Walt Disney, Buena Vista, Lyric Street, and Hollywood Records in its stable of recording labels.

First up, Team Hilary decided the best way to test the waters was to insert a song by Hilary on the official soundtrack to *Lizzie McGuire*, which was scheduled to be released by Walt Disney Records on August 13, 2002. The song chosen was called "I Can't Wait," and it was a very straightforward, young-skewing pop record with a highly infectious "bum-bum-bum" refrain. It had a Wilson Phillips vibe, and it became a sensation on Radio Disney, where to this day it is often still in the Top 30 playlist.

Hilary was proud of "I Can't Wait," and was thrilled to be on her way toward a proper recording career. "I had never recorded a song before, so I didn't know what to expect. It turned out to be fun, but a lot of hard work, too. Overall, I'm really proud of what I was able to accomplish my first time out."

She told *Popstar!* that she was rushed when it came to selecting "I Can't Wait," but that she felt it turned out great. She also loved a dance remix of the track that was commissioned.

Hilary's first effort was a home run. Not only was it a good song in its own right but it was also the highest-profile song on *The Lizzie McGuire Soundtrack*, which earned a gold record—that's 500,000-plus copies in sales—Hilary's first!

"I found out when I was running to do a scene so I didn't have time to really think about it till later that night, and I was like, 'Oh, my God . . . I went gold!'"

Hilary also contributed "The Tiki, Tiki Room" to the first *Disneymania* collection, and plunged into recording a Christmas album as a next step toward expressing herself fully as a singer.

Santa Claus Lane was Hilary's first full-length studio album. It contained exuberant recordings of classic holiday tunes and some new stuff, too, including duets with major R&B stars Lil' Romeo and Christina Milian.

Thanks to the wonders of modern technology, she didn't even *meet* her duet partner Lil' Romeo until they filmed the video for the song "Tell Me a Story (About the Night Before)," which had become a Radio Disney favorite.

Over time, *Santa Claus Lane* also went gold—her first full-length album to achieve 500,000-plus in sales.

Hilary's next step was to prepare for a major-label debut, which would occur August 26, 2003, via Hollywood Records.

During an MSN chat, Hilary responded to a fan's question about making her next album by saying, "Recording an album was totally different than recording in a studio [for *Santa Claus Lane*]. It's hard . . . but I have great people around me that help me find music that I really like."

One great person to have around her was Andre Recke. His experience with Myra had led him to a fast friendship with a trio of writers and producers—Lauren Christy, Graham Edwards, and Scott Spock—who go by the collective name of The Matrix. By the time Hilary was cutting her first mainstream-pop album, The Matrix had just scored by crafting the sound of Avril Lavigne. They were the hot creative crew of 2003, and they already had a great relationship with Andre—he would not have to struggle to get them to consider contributing songs for his newcomer.

Hilary was becoming a mega-star thanks to the squeaky-clean *Lizzie McGuire*, so most of her fans expected her to deliver pure pop. Before her album came out, she fulfilled the bubblegum dreams of some fans with "Why Not," a song that appeared (along with "What Dreams Are Made Of") on the sound track for *The Lizzie McGuire Movie*. This gem was ten times the hit that "I Can't Wait" had been, and got Hilary the attention of MTV and *TRL*. She was perfectly positioned for her CD to come out in August.

"If the pixie dust flies the right way," Buena Vista Music Group chairman Bob Cavallo told *Billboard*, "I expect we'll sell a couple of million." Big talk—but it wound up being a conservative estimate.

Making the album was not easy, but it was personally satisfying to Hilary. She later said on her DVD *Hilary Duff: All Access Pass*, "When you're acting, you're putting yourself in someone else's shoes. It not about you at all. But when you're singing in the studio, it's all about you. It's really personal."

The most surprising thing to critics about Hilary's album *Metamorphosis* is just how well it turned out. As I told Hilary in Hawaii right after its release, she was popular enough that if she had wanted to, she could have thrown together a really weak CD and cashed in. But Hilary would not hear of it. She, Andre, and Susan made sure that the album would show Hilary's true personality—as distinct from Lizzie—and would prove she was beginning to move into the young adult phase of her career.

"You know, I took a really, really long time working on the album, and I took a long time to put the CD together because I was so crazy; I wanted *everything* to be perfect, and *every* song I wanted to relate to, and I wanted to have something that I could be really proud of instead of just throwing something together that I know I could, you know, do and sell a couple records."

At only fifteen, Hilary delivered an album with songs that would make kids happy, would seem cool to teens, and would even reel in adults. Once, a couple in their forties sent a fan note to Hilary on an airplane to tell her they loved rocking out to her songs in their car every day!

The title *Metamorphosis* was suggested both by Hilary's musical growth and her acting growth—not to mention the fact that she had gone from being a kid to being a beautiful, confident young woman. She had begun writing songs in 2002 and one of her earliest efforts—rewritten and revamped by pro Chico Bennett—had become the album track "Metamorphosis," even more reason to christen the album with that mouthful of a title.

"Change is a very important and natural thing. We called the album *Metamorphosis* because it's about changes that everybody experiences. It's not just about me, but it's very personal. This music is a good way to get everyone to know the real me."

Hilary loved all her collaborators on *Metamorphosis* and gushed about them to the press. Perhaps her most beloved was Haylie Duff!

"Since she knows me better than anyone else in the world," Hilary said, "Haylie wrote 'Sweet Sixteen,' a really fun song that totally relates to my life right now. She also came up with 'Inner Strength,' and it's really beautiful. Very empowering and uplifting."

The album was pop, but it was carefully infused with rock elements.

"The music on the album is a little different from the pop songs everyone's heard from me before, because *Metamorphosis* has all the kinds of music I like to listen to. There are a lot of different sounds, from rock to electronic—with a whole range of tempos from some deep, slow songs, to some high-energy rock songs to give me a boost. Everybody goes through different moods and different feelings and sometimes when you put on your favorite song it makes you feel a little bit better."

Hilary's lead single from *Metamorphosis* was "So Yesterday," a Matrix project that she didn't even *like* when she first heard a demo! Hilary tried to dissuade Andre from including it on her record, but he lobbied hard and once she had sung it and heard the final cut, she knew it would be a smash hit.

"So Yesterday" became a number-one-selling single and garnered slow-burn airplay for months on end. It ignited MTV's interest—the video was given a *Making the Video* segment that aired the week of July 2 and she cohosted a *TRL All-Star Backyard BBQ with Carson Daly* that aired Sunday, July 13, 2003.

The "So Yesterday" video—Hilary's first proper music video after the thrown-together clips for songs like "I Can't Wait," "Tell Me a Story (About the Night Before)," and "Why Not"—found her playing a revenge-seeker who tortures her playa ex by stealing his shirt and having it worn by a variety of freaks on Venice Beach. The odd story line was fresh and seemed real to kids, who made it a huge *TRL* request.

Metamorphosis was released August 26, 2003, at the height of the popularity of "So Yesterday." It debuted at number two, selling over 200,000 units, and it wound up on top of the charts the following week. Hilary was elated by the instant acceptance, but she knew that her success in music, just like her success in acting, was not as "overnight" as it appeared to casual observers. She had put in the hard work and now she was reaping the rewards.

Her second single, "Come Clean," was every bit as powerful as "So Yesterday" had been. With the song's lyrical depth and Hilary's mature vocal, "Come Clean," became one of the most-played songs of 2003. Its video was also very grown-up. Director Dave Meyers told *J-14* magazine, "I tried to do something where you're taking her very seriously. . . . I don't think we've ever seen this from her. She's been a bit of a pop icon, so I'm just trying to give her a bit more credibility on an artist front." The song was even used as the theme for MTV's reality show *Laguna Beach.*

Hilary had displayed her musical side in films, on the radio, and on MTV. All that was left was to perform a concert on a major network.

In the summer of 2003, Hilary journeyed to the Hawaiian island of Kauai with her parents, her sister, her best friends, her management team, and of course her newly formed band. She filmed a TV special for The WB to be entitled *Hilary Duff's Island Birthday Bash,* which was aired September 24 and September 28 (her "sweet sixteen" birthday).

For the special, Hilary filmed unique, music-videolike clips in remote locations and also allowed herself to be filmed scuba diving, fishing, swimming, riding all-terrain vehicles, and doing other things that any tourist would do. The centerpiece of the trip was a lengthy concert—Hilary's very first!—containing the songs of *Metamorphosis* and featuring Simple Plan as an opening act. She became fast friends with the band.

Hilary has said "Come Clean" is her favorite of all her videos!

Hilary enjoyed having her entire original band not only on the set but in the video!

The atmosphere making "Come Clean" was totally relaxed—Hilary was among friends!

Her white boots and matching fuzzy sweater paired with jeans created a fashion craze at many schools!

Hilary was at her most grown-up in this video, looking like the glamorous movie star she actually is!

A victorious Hilary and partner Alex won the kayak race, but it was a struggle with so much competition! The photographer had to stand in the water to get these shots!

As these shots show, Hilary was genuinely surprised when her friends presented her with a scrapbook of the entire special!

Hilary with her beloved coach and friend Troy in a rare slow moment during the ATV adventure!

The concert showed how far Hilary had come from her first singing lessons. She sang well and had a command of the stage—she looked as if she'd been singing her whole life! The local kids who were allowed in to the concert free went wild.

The *New York Times*, in reviewing Hilary's work at this time, pointed out that "Ms. Duff actually makes being a teenager look and sound like fun."

Hilary would take her fun act on the road with two successful national concert tours and an international jaunt that found her wowing fans in Japan, Australia, and Europe.

"My shows are more like rock concerts. I don't really dance. They're not choreographed. We jump around onstage and have a lot of energy."

For her next musical venture, Hilary was adamant that she wanted to make more of a creative contribution than she had with *Metamorphosis*. Already, she had done more than many first-time singers do. But Hilary wanted to do more than merely direct—she wanted to help create her musical destiny.

During the making of *Metamorphosis*, Hilary had expressed discomfort with songwriting, at least in respect to crafting a whole song from scratch with an eye toward the overall form. But post-*Metamorphosis*, she told *Billboard* that she loved writing. "I feel like you need time to really get in touch with yourself to do that." For *Metamorphosis*, she said, she "would have liked to have had more time to work with the writers [and] write some more of my own stuff. Hopefully, I can do that on my second album."

Her dreams were realized with her next record, the lengthy (seventeen tracks!) and more complex *Hilary Duff*, released on her birthday in 2004.

"I no longer relate to lollipops," she famously told a reporter from *Blender* as she posed for the music magazine's October 2004 cover. The material on *Hilary Duff* reflects her maturation from the cute kid who only a year earlier had pluckily sung "Why Not."

"Compared to the first album, when I wasn't confident enough to make suggestions, this time around, I was very involved. If I thought it needed to be more heavy, more rock, I said so."

Why would she name the album after herself this time?

"I feel that this record is so much more me."

Hilary's lead single was the gorgeous "Fly," a song she called "uplifting" for its urging to be positive in the face of all the negativity in the world.

"It's about how people are scared to open up and show who they are inside because they're afraid of what others are going to say."

Fans embraced the new, more grown-up Hilary because she was acting her age, not *beyond* her age, as some thought her idol Britney Spears had done.

Both Hilary and Haylie have creative credits on *Hilary Duff*, and there is every sign that Hilary's songwriting will only expand over the course of her career.

Haylie's song "Mr. James Dean" came off as a juicy tell-off to an ex-boyfriend. "James Dean was great, but this person was a poser," Hilary said.

But the album's most controversial track was "Haters," a stinging rebuke against a female rival that Hilary and Haylie collaborated on. The media immediately assumed it might be directed at Lindsay Lohan, but Hilary laughs off the idea that she would write a song about Lindsay.

Hilary herself has said she adores "Who's That Girl?" ("I cried when I first heard the song!") and "Weird," which she felt was a major departure. She has said of "Underneath This Smile" that it *is* her life.

Touchingly, the CD's booklet contains a scan of Hilary's autograph with the inscription, "To my fans, I dedicate it all to you, Love, Hil."

With her musical career firmly established, Hilary Duff seems to have conquered the entertainment world from top to bottom. She seems almost like a goddess to her biggest fans, but Hilary has never put on airs. She sees herself as "very normal!"

In late 2004, she told Australia's *New Weekly* that she is comfortable with her entire career, with the choices she's made, and with living in her own skin.

"People can be very judgmental," she conceded. "I'm a little bit older so I laugh it off and don't really pay attention to it. I have an incredibly supportive family and we're very close and normal."

Speaking of family, perhaps that is the final frontier for Hilary, something she will tackle as she gets (much!) older.

When *People* magazine asked her to speculate about where she would be in a decade, then-fifteen-year-old Hilary exclaimed, "I want a family. Oh, my God! I'm going to be twenty-five in ten years!"

Hilary already has her own loving family, as well as the wide circle of fans who consider her to be like family already. She is the normal girl with the abnormal amount of talent, energy, and drive.

After years of trying to make it, Hilary has gained her "All Access" pass in Hollywood—and in the hearts of her many admirers.

Quiz

Can You Do the Musical Math?

1. What 1980s song did Hilary and Haylie remake for the soundtrack of *A Cinderella Story*?

2. Which Hil song asserts, "I believe all things are possible on Christmas Eve"?

3. Besides Hilary (*Lizzie McGuire*), who makes up the Disney Channel Circle of Stars?

4. In what song does Hilary sing that she cries like a baby if she doesn't get her way?

5. Kara DioGuardi and John Shanks wrote what mega-hit from Hilary's *Metamorphosis* CD?

What song was Hilary singing at the precipice of Waimea Canyon?

6. In The WB's special *Hilary Duff's Island Birthday Bash,* which song did she sing at Waimea Canyon?

7. What Walt Disney's *Lady and the Tramp* song did Hilary remake for the *Disneymania 2* CD?

8. Name the two items of clothing Hilary tells her ex-boyfriend she is going to keep in the song "So Yesterday."

9. What song does Hilary sing two versions of in *The Lizzie McGuire Movie*?

10. Hilary said which hard-to-sing song from *Metamorphosis* was about her conscience?

Answers

1. "Our Lips Are Sealed"
2. "Tell Me a Story (About the Night Before)"
3. Christy Carlson Romano (*Kim Possible* and *Even Stevens*); A. J. Trauth (*Even Stevens*); Raven-Symoné, Anneliese van der Pol, and Orlando Brown (*That's So Raven*); and Tahj Mowry (*Smart Guy* and *Kim Possible*)
4. "Do You Want Me?"
5. "Come Clean."
6. "Anywhere but Here"
7. "The Siamese Cat Song," with Haylie Duff
8. "Your Jeans and Your Old Black Hat"
9. "What Dreams Are Made Of"
10. "Little Voice"

Workin' It Out

All-Around Hilary

Hilary Duff

Hilary has known Kids
With A Cause prez,
Linda Finnegan, since
1998—they share a
passion for helping to
improve kids' lives!

Kid With A Cause: Why Hilary Duff Believes in Giving Back—And How She Does It!

Many stars donate their time and their money toward charitable causes. But rather than using her charity work to shape and enhance her "image," Hilary Duff has been actively involved in helping others—with her mother, Susan, as a role model—since before she was famous.

Hilary's biggest charitable commitment is to Kids With A Cause (kidswithacause.org). This organization was launched in September 1999 to help children "who, through no fault of their own, suffer from poverty, hunger, sickness, lack of education, abandonment, neglect and/or abuse." Its members are young performers with a strong desire to help those less fortunate than themselves.

Hilary and Haylie were charter members of Kids With A Cause, having met its director Linda Finnegan in 1998 when she was executive director of the Audrey Hepburn Children Fund and the Duffs were on the advisory board.

"I love Linda—she is such an inspiration!" Hilary told reporter Renee Rodrigues. "I love kids and giving back. It really makes me feel special."

The charity does countless things to help children, including hosting an annual Oscars party, gatherings where kids get to meet stars like Hilary, visits by stars to children's hospitals, field trips to theme parks, and many other fund-raisers. They've collaborated on fulfilling wishes with Make-A-Wish and have even done pet rescues!

Hilary has made personal appearances to benefit the cause, designed T-shirts (angelwear.com), been involved in a "Send a Greeting by Phone" drive and performed at a charity event at the House of Blues in Los Angeles.

Hilary believes in giving back because, as she succinctly told *Teen Vogue*, "I get so much that other girls don't."

"Our parents taught us it's the little things you can do that can make such a big improvement in our lives as well as the lives of others," Hilary said.

Susan Duff told *Cowboys & Indians* magazine, "In life, you have to turn out to be a good citizen. The success doesn't matter. Who knows how long it's going to last? The real thing is how you're going to get through life and contribute."

Another charity close to Hilary's heart is Return to Freedom (returntofreedom.org). This organization is dedicated to saving wild horses. Its mission is informed by the Henry David Thoreau quote, "In wildness is the preservation of the world."

Hilary visited the California grounds in July of 2003, when she met RTF's founder, Neda DeMayo, and learned of the great suffering endured by wild horses.

She was grateful for the opportunity to meet Spirit, the now-famous horse used as a stepping-off point for the 2002 DreamWorks feature *Spirit: Stallion of the Cimarron.*

Hilary was quoted as saying, "I had to catch my breath when I saw him . . . he's, like, *stunning!*"

On her role as a youth ambassador, Hilary seems to feel humbled more than anything.

"I'm so honored," she announced in a press release. "It's so important to raise the awareness of other kids and that's the best part of being in the position I'm in. I think it's really important to give back to your community and it makes you feel so good to get involved with a charity. So when I first heard about Return to Freedom, and how civilization is closing in on the wild mustangs, I knew that I wanted to get involved with this cause. It is so great that the mustangs have the American Wild Horse Sanctuary at Return to Freedom to roam free on and to be wild. If their land and freedom is lost, these wild horses are in real danger of becoming extinct and we must not let that happen. I hope that Return to Freedom will be able to get more land so that they can rescue and bring more horses to the sanctuary."

Hilary's passion for this organization—and for all of Mother Nature's creatures—led her to create an entire line of doggie clothes and accessories named for her own late, great pet. Sales from all Little Dog Duff Stuff merchandise benefit Return to Freedom and dog-rescue charities.

Some people might look down on charitable endeavors as evidence of Hilary being a Goody Two-shoes. Nothing could be more uncool than attempting to belittle something done from the heart.

Karen Bradford, who knew Hilary in her earliest days in Los Angeles, sums up why anyone who's jealous of Hilary's success should consider Hilary's character. After Hilary had become a huge star, Karen was able to tell Hilary how proud she was of all she'd accomplished.

"She did her usual—she started laughing and smiling. So when you see that sweet smile on that beautiful young kid, I know personally that it belongs to someone who I am pleased and happy to see has succeeded beyond anyone's wildest dreams. I hope her star continues to shine in the most positive and sincerest way."

Why Not? Hilary Hits a Home-Run with Stuff by Hilary Duff!

By now, if you've been following Hilary's brilliant career closely, you know that she is the type of girl to "take a crazy chance." This is exactly what she did in developing her own brand.

Mary-Kate Olsen and her sister, Ashley Olsen, had already shown that a multimillion-dollar brand targeted solely at a tween and teen market could be built around very young stars. In 2003, it was Hilary's turn to try her hand at using her name to help sell products she loves and believes in and—in some cases—helps conceive!

Hilary told *USA Today,* "It's weird that my name would be on something and make someone want to buy it. It's crazy, because I'm such a normal teenager."

In 2003, Hilary teamed up with a top-notch licensing company to launch Stuff by Hilary Duff, an extensive line of products that included clothing, cosmetics, jewelry, shoes, furniture, bedding and beach accessories, posters, calendars, stickers, and much more. She even teamed up with Visa for a series of her very own gift cards!

Hilary's products connect with their intended audience not only because they're quality items that speak to kids' everyday needs and appeal to their imaginations but also because Hilary's own taste is perfectly suited to the tastes of other people her age.

As long as Hilary embodies what's cool, Stuff by Hilary Duff's sales will continue to be red-hot!

"I think everything you wear reflects your mood . . . even if other people don't notice it!"

Passion for Fashion: How to Capture Hilary's Killer Style!

Hilary is *the* fashion plate of her generation. She has always displayed impeccable taste and an ingenuity with her style that has made her someone to look up—and *dress up*—to!

Check out some of her best looks and then follow this handy guide for how to re-create them. Hilary does not necessarily endorse the items suggested, but not everyone has the money to wear designer clothes. Even Hilary herself used to enjoy taking her old stuff and ripping it up and making it into something new.

Get creative, get fashionable . . . get started!

Fashion Faves!

In general, Hilary adores scoop-neck and tank tops (long and short), capris, anything with an '80s vibe, and denim, denim, denim. Some of her fave designers are Fiorucci, Calvin Klein, Prada, Pierre Hardy, and Nicole Miller! Lately, she totally loves Rock & Republic for jeans!

Making Up Is Easy to Do!

For makeup that will help you achieve a Hilary Duff look, try townleycosmetics.com for the full line of Stuff by Hilary Duff goodies! Outside her own line, Hilary loves Mario Badescu Enzyme Cleansing Gel for keeping her face clean and spot-free. She insists she has no set faves, but has in the past used Lancôme Juicy Tubes and lip glosses by Nars. She's also used BeneFit, Hard Candy, Tony & Tina, and MAC. Her single greatest makeup signature of late? Heavily kohled eyes—that smoky look is very now!

Hair Apparent!

"I like bangs because they're versatile!" Hilary told *Girls' Life* of her signature 'do. The key to mimicking her long hairstyle is to "condition, condition, condition!" That keeps hair heavy and straight like Hil's usually is.

Hilary Duff

Rock the Looks!

Use this section to take all of the guesswork out of capturing Hilary's unique style!

Calendar Girl!

The Basics! This sporty look—one popularized by Hilary in her official calendar and on a hot-selling poster—has a vibe similar to Stuff by Hilary Duff's World Traveler line, about which Hilary says, "My World Traveler line is inspired by cities I've been to all over the globe!" The look is a simple one to make! The key is to find **just the right striped top** and pair it with either your **comfiest jeans** or even **a denim skirt.** Inspired by Hilary's World Traveler line, this look has an '80s vibe. To preserve that feel, keep your top red and white, pink and black, or pink and white!

Rockstar!

The Basics! Hilary's onstage persona is characterized by a snug **black tank** and a pair of the coolest, slim-fitting **black jeans** around. She will pair this midnight combo with **black or black-and-white boots** in leather or in soft suede, the higher the better. You can achieve this exact look every time with just those three elements! Have fun messing up your hair for this look!

Casual Cool!

The Basics! This look is easily created using staples of just about any girl's wardrobe. First, start with a **white tank or T** and add a **loose sweater in an Easter-egg color**— pale pink, lilac, or seafoam green. Choose **lived-in jeans** and bottom out with **sandals** for an overall chill look that even those ultraperfect *OC* girls will envy!

It's a Wrap!

The Basics! Every girl likes to make a dramatic entrance and catch a little attention, right? Well, some girls make the mistake of showing too much skin or wearing eye-popping colors and mismatched patterns to create a scene. With this look, Hilary shows that sometimes, all it takes is one piece of clothing to make everyone take notice. A punchy **poncho in a rich, vibrant color** is striking, mysterious . . . and warm! It makes you feel safe and protected, too, not to mention that it's a terrific way to preserve modesty.

Kid Stuff!

The Basics! This carefree, youthful look is about as close as you can get to the Stuff by Hilary Duff line without being a part of it. To match it, find a **solid top with a feminine bow or tie** and **polka-dotted or white capris.** The **sky blue–hued shoes** are key components—these heels take the outfit from the playground to being right for a hot all-ages club!

Arrivederci, Lizzie!

Around the time of *The Lizzie McGuire Movie*, Hilary flaunted this grown-up take on the character's juvenile style. It's still a hot look on the tween scene today, so to build your own, you just need to focus on two major elements. First, you gotta get a **pastel cap**! You can get a look-alike to this one or try a beret. The **loose print top** is the other target, preferably one with flowy, fluttery sleeves. All you need to finish things up would be any kind of jeans or dark pants. Shoes? Up to you!

T-Time!

Hilary, like fashionistas of all ages, loves a good **message T**! You can find one in a vintage store (look for '80s prints with Patrick Nagel art like old-time band Duran Duran's *Rio* album cover to closely match Hil's "So Yesterday" top) or at mass retailers like Gap, Abercrombie & Fitch, Kmart, or Bebe. Wherever you shop, you'll find a back-talking top! If you want the exact Kids With A Cause T Hilary wears in the pic below with Lyndsy Fonseca, you can buy yours at kidswithacause.org and help a very worthy cause!

The Chanteuse!

To look like a sophisticated songstress, Hil uses a **crest-print black top** to create a foundation that is neat and yet still has enough flair to imply a stage is in her near future. **Ankle-high black boots** are smart rather than flashy, leaving **vertical-striped pants** to do all the attention getting. These slacks make a performer visible from a mile away and also make legs look that much longer!

Island Princess!

Of course, this is not a good look for school. But for the beach or for a pool party, this look is not only easy to do, it's fun! You should start with an **animal-print bathing suit or bikini.** Cheetah is one of Hil's fave animal prints, but you can also consider others, like zebra. Just avoid cow print. I mean, it's a bathing suit, y'know? Hilary's brown wrap picks up the cheetah hue and covers up her legs both to keep the look parent-friendly and to make it adaptable to evening splash fests when the sun is in retreat. The most "Hilary Duff" aspect of this look would be the turquoise **geometric earrings**—they pick up the strap of her suit and set off her face beautifully. To look like Hil, look for anything '80s and create unexpected contrasts! And as for footwear . . . what footwear?

Ski Bunny!

Hil's "Come Clean" vid look was one of her most grown-up—and her fans loved it! Luckily, it's easy to do on your own for not much moola. Everyone's got jeans, so you're good to go on the bottom. **Knee-high white boots** are more of an investment, but you need to have a pair of good boots—and you could potentially find a pair that works with both this look and the rock star look from this section. On top, you want a warm, comfy, **off-the-shoulder sweater** in white or ivory. A similar look can be achieved with a **turtleneck,** depending on the temperature outside. This look works for school or a party and is one of Hilary's most widely copied.

Cali Cowgirl!

One of Hil's cutest, newest looks is this combo that's a little bit Texas, a little bit L.A.—and all Hilary Duff! Build it with a simple **camo tank** and your most used-and-abused **distressed jeans.** You'll want a **brown suede belt**—whether functional or just for show—and matching **boots.** If you can't find a suitable **mini jacket** like Hilary has, you can improvise by cutting up a **men's tan work shirt**—leave the edges ragged! Once your dad gives you one, you just cut it to the right length and then cut the front so only a bit of material remains at the arms and in the back. The key to finishing this look is to layer yourself with **silver necklaces** and **funky bracelets.** Earthy stuff only—no plastic, no rubber bands. Stick to **turquoise Santa Fe jewelry** or even simple leather straps at the wrist.

Substance over Style!

Yes, Hilary loves clothes and cares about her appearance, but she's also not one of those girls who *only* cares about what the label says. She told Australia's *New Weekly* magazine, "I don't go out to parties—seriously, if there's a *Teen Vogue* party on or a bunch of my friends hanging out in my friend's apartment and I've got the night off, I'm going to go to my friend's apartment. I work so much and I'd rather not go someplace where people are going to look me up and down and see what kinds of shoes I'm wearing."

Hilary's Number One Fashion Tip!

Hilary told *Life Story,* "I . . . want kids to feel really good about themselves and to know that they won't have to show off a lot of skin to be pretty or cool!"

Hilary
24/7

Total Access!

Hilary is always busy, but
she still takes time out to
have fun!

A Day in the Sun: Check Out a Day in the Life of Hilary!

While she was filming *Lizzie McGuire* episodes, Hilary told the *National Enquirer* her schedule included a 5:30 A.M. wake-up from her mom, Susan, a shower, getting dressed, doing homework, taking care of her doggies, and then going to work on the set.

"We stop and get chicken fingers and dipping sauce. Then I come to the set and get made up and go to wardrobe and hair. I do a couple of scenes and go to school with a thirty-minute break for lunch."

After the series wrap of *Lizzie McGuire*, Hilary's daily schedule was something like this:

- school for four hours
- voice class for two hours
- recording studio for four to six hours
- phone interviews, talk-show appearances, and photo shoots when possible during the day

Hilary told *YM* magazine that her schedule was filled with normal, everyday things as well as glamorous premieres.

"After work, I go home and do my homework, hang with friends, and take out the trash. It's weird when people ask me for my autograph or freak when they see me, because I'm just like them."

Practice Makes Perfect!

Hilary spends hours a day rehearsing when she's leading up to a tour. Here, she's hangin' with her way-cool musical director, Ty Stevens!

Fan Fun!

Meet-and-greets with fans are crucial to any performer's popularity. Hilary does them at every concert because she truly appreciates her biggest supporters!

Record-Breaking Record-Making!

Working on her last two CDs, Hilary had to devote hours from most of her days to the studio. Here, she works on <u>Metamorphosis</u>—with a smile!

Shopping Without Dropping!

Hilary's multitalented, but one of her greatest skills isn't marketable—she's a world-class shopper! She's shopped New York, L.A., Toronto, Vancouver, Tokyo, Paris, London, Rome, and beyond! If she has any downtime in a city she happens to be in, she'll give the stores a run for <u>her</u> money!

83

The Power of Pals!
Hilary is not a star who forgets
her buddies—she makes them
an important part of her day!
Hilary loves going for breakfast
or coffee with her friends and
just being a normal teenager.
Here, she hangs with friends
Alex and Eliana on a break
from shopping!

Strike a Pose!

Photo shoots are par for the course for any performer. Hilary often gets to choose her own hair and makeup people. Back in the old days . . . she used to do her own!

School's Cool!

Even though she managed to avoid a typical school setting after the age of ten, schoolwork is a major part of Hilary's life. The law requires that young performers get a set amount of study time every single day. Also, Hilary does plan to attend college one day . . . so you do "The Math"!

85

All Things Hilary for Her Biggest Fans!

Hilaryscopes!: Learn About Your Sign and Find Out If You Could Hang with Hil!

Check out these insights into your mind and predictions for your future—with a totally Duff-centric vibe!

Aries

> The Ram (Fire)
> March 21–April 19
> **Personal Power Color: Red**
> **Most Compatible Signs: Leo and Sagittarius**

The Big Picture

This sign is blessed with courage—you're likely to be someone who is thought of as fearless or even pioneering. This means you not only cook up great ideas, you have no problem doing whatever it takes to execute them. You also tend to attract followers in much the same way a star (like Hilary) would—except your boosters follow you out of a shared sense of mission instead of idolizing you. In relation to your fandom of Hilary Duff, you might already be an on-line Street Team leader or the president of one of her local fan clubs. If not—give it a thought! Another aspect of your leadership ability is your penchant for exploring. Just be sure you balance your desire to discover new things and to get to the bottom of minimysteries with tact and smarts. You take flight often, but you always take a parachute with you!

Special Powers

Your greatest powers are those of persuasion. You persuade not in a lawyerly way, by argument, but in an exemplary way. You're someone who is able to change minds simply by being yourself and doing your thing. You sometimes do it so easily it can almost rise to an apparently magical level in the eyes of observers. It ain't magic, though, it's just plain old charisma!

Things to Do

Some work you have to do on your personality would include overcoming selfishness and vanity. Don't even pretend these are not problems you've already noticed in yourself, and don't get mad—Arians sometimes exist in a constant state of agitation if they don't watch it. Practice anger management at the same time you practice self-control when it comes to risk taking. Also, try to be extra mindful of others' feelings—your strong sense of security sometimes leads to an abrasive streak.

Your Future

You do not have a sterling future in a business partnership. But the good news is that you are destined to achieve on an executive level and in self-reliant positions. You're great at delegating and supervising responsibility. Your skill in these areas, as well as your quick wit, should make you a revered and respected point person.

Taurus

The Bull (Earth)
April 20–May 20
Personal Power Color: Mauve
Most Compatible Signs: Virgo and Capricorn

The Big Picture

Taureans are the Rock of Gibraltar, meaning you're the most reliable person to have on any team, whether it's a basketball squad or just a circle of friends. You're the person people come to with secrets and for advice because you're evenhanded and consistent and you take the time to weigh all sides. You're a great problem solver, a characteristic that is matched by your industrious attitude toward work, schoolwork, and also hobbies, which tend to be serious kinds of pursuits (like sculpting) more so than tension relievers (like collecting bottle caps).

Special Powers

Your greatest power is that of seeing the big picture. You're able to contextualize everything and to issue a very commonsense outlook on any situation. You're openminded, but your take on any given dilemma is black and white—and often totally correct.

Things to Do

You should spice up your day-to-day life as you tend toward the—dare I say it?—boring! Not like majorly yawn inducing, but more of a stuck-in-a-rut way. Friends need to be reminded you're not just a dispute resolver, you're also a young, fun, exciting person. Work on your patience with people who don't get the real you. Cut them slack because you're more complex than even *you* realize at this point.

Your Future

Regardless of what you do to earn a living, make sure it has to do with weighing facts. You'd make a terrific judge or detective, but you'd also be excellent as a consultant of any kind in whatever area strikes your fancy. A banker? Right on the money! You're quite materialistic—a trait to downplay where possible—so it should excite you to know there is no reason you can't wind up with a bank account as fat as Hilary Duff's! You're very loving by nature, so all your future romances are likely to be characterized by over-the-top gestures, gifts, pledges, and signs on your part—and you're likely to seek the same in return.

Gemini

The Twins (Air)
May 21–June 20
Personal Power Color: Yellow
Most Compatible Signs: Libra (Hil's sign!) and Aquarius

The Big Picture

Every expert agrees that Geminis are superb at communication. You're a terrific speaker and writer, both creatively and journalistically. You probably keep a diary. If not, you should! Friends love your e-mails and may look to you for the juiciest roundup of all the latest gossip. You're vibrant, full of life, and also pretty brainy. People think of you as extremely entertaining, either to talk to or to go to concerts and special events with. You probably get invited to lots of birthday parties, where you often wind up being more fun than pin the tail on the donkey. Gemini is the sign of the twins, so you probably have a dual nature. You may be the life of the party but you're also introspective, or the most talkative person in your class but quiet and shy in new situations. On the downside, you could be accused of being a little flighty—though that is easy enough to . . . like . . . *overcome,* man.

Special Powers

Your power to communicate is nothing to sneeze at. You're dependable and mature, too, and the combo makes you someone who is considered to be an authority. You're like Hilary, who as a teen is a little adult in her head.

Things to Do

You need to work on your fickle nature—you can sometimes be distracted by silly pursuits (here's where that flightiness comes in) and that can lead to hurt feelings in your relationships. Try to channel your nervous energy into self-improving pursuits, like stress reduction and personality tests. Above all, when you start a new pursuit, follow it through—at all costs. You cannot afford to be one of those people who start a million projects and finish none. Take Hilary as your guide and develop some of her strength.

Your Future

You're *so* going to be in a field involving communications—this may include the obvious, such as writing for a teen magazine or publishing a newspaper, or it may be less obvious, such as creating jingles for TV commercials. You may also be a good candidate for education, politics, or even as a religious or spiritual leader. If you avoid the dark side of your skills (for example, you'd make a great scammer in one of those hard-to-believe infomercials!), you should have no problem achieving success.

Cancer

The Crab (Water)
June 21–July 22
Personal Power Color: Blue-green
Most Compatible Signs: Scorpio and Pisces

The Big Picture

Many of the signs need to work on being more sensitive—this is not your problem! Your nature is that of a very caring, nurturing person. You might seem motherly or big-sisterly (or big-brotherly!) to people, even those who are your age or older. This is because of your warm heart—it's so warm strangers can sense it on their first meetings with you. You're patriotic and you tend to become caught up in emotionally charged causes. Friends often admire you even if they don't openly admit it—you represent the kind of person they feel they *should* be, but aren't.

Special Powers

Your best attribute is your calming nature. In a crisis, you will be the person to quiet any hysteria with a few sensible words and a steely exterior. You're able to weather all of life's storms—and there will be some—with grace and dignity, and with a strong survival instinct.

Things to Do

You do need to take some time out to examine why you allow people's actions to bother you so deeply. You're likely to be the kind of person to take great offense at things others would not even interpret as slights. Do you find yourself being mad at friends without them knowing it? Sometimes this may be because they are insensitive. But other times, it's *you* who are being *overly* sensitive.

Your Future

You would be an amazing doctor, nurse, veterinarian, or naturalist. Like Hilary, you probably dig animals and would do anything to protect the defenseless animals (and people) in this world. One possible future career could be in a humanitarian field, like working for the Red Cross or for a charity like the ones Hilary supports. You would also make a seriously in-demand chef. Use your highly developed imagination—there is no limit to what you can achieve when you allow yourself to let go of your perceptions of your limitations.

Leo

The Lion (Fire)
July 23–August 22
Personal Power Color: Gold
Most Compatible Signs: Aries and Sagittarius

The Big Picture

"Big" is right! You've got a huge personality and are probably someone who's been in school plays or performed in public in other ways. Leos are known to be magnetic entertainers (like Hilary!) who are multitalented and who are not shy about sharing their gifts. You're also creative (you might not only sing but write your own stuff) and inquisitive. You might be a big spender, too, and are probably the first person to hand a dollar to a beggar on the street.

Special Powers

You know what they are already—you can sing, dance, act, and/or make people laugh. You might also be a skillful creative writer. Whatever your particular standout ability is, you're probably so good at it that everyone who knows you knows about this ability. You're also a born leader.

Things to Do

You need to avoid believing your own hype. Sure, everyone thinks you're amazing, and you are, but don't let that make you bigheaded or smug. People like exuberant entertainers and dislike show-offs. Try to soften your bossy nature and open your mind to those around you who may be totally different personality types.

Your Future

You're a born star, whether of Hilary's level or maybe just on a local level. Either way, follow your dream and be the best you can. Avoid settling and doing whatever comes easiest because with just a little extra work, you can be not only good but great.

Virgo

The Virgin (Earth)
August 23–September 22
Personal Power Color: Green
Most Compatible Signs: Taurus and Capricorn

The Big Picture

You're very practical in everything you do, and very thoughtful. You would rather think things through cautiously than jump feet-first into situations that may or may not turn out for the best. You're anything but ego driven—in fact, all your accomplishments tend to be modestly hidden from view. You like order and organization and are probably thought of as neat and grounded.

Special Powers

Your organizational skills are second to none. This means you're great at math (even the dreaded story problems), cards, and at solving mysteries. You probably love and excel at word and number games. You're not just an egghead, though, you're also a fashion plate who knows a lot about personal style in the same way Hilary Duff does.

Things to Do

One thing you need to soften is your critical nature. You tend to come off as a bit harsh, especially if you react irritably when your criticisms are rejected. Still, your analytical nature should make confronting any personal problems you have a piece of cake.

Your Future

You would make a superb event organizer thanks not only to your ability to multitask but also to your endless energy. You're not bubbly and effervescent, you're more indefatigable. People may consider you an Energizer bunny. You're careful with money (cheap, cough-cough) so would be a terrific treasurer in any organization. An obvious career path for you would be editing the work of others (whether in writing or design or in overseeing financial work), but a less obvious, and potentially more rewarding, route would be to consider anything involving history.

Libra

The Scales (Air)
September 23–October 22
Personal Power Color: Blue
Most Compatible Signs: Gemini and Aquarius

The Big Picture

If you're a Libra, you share that with the girl this book is written about—Hilary Erhard Duff was born September 28! Let's start with the good news. Libras represent the most diplomatic of all the signs, meaning you're a great peacemaker among your friends and family. You've never met anyone you don't like, and even better, no one you've met has ever disliked you! You're also likely to be quite the romantic ('fess up . . . you have posters of some heartthrob on your wall, right?) both in love and in other aspects of life. You like to look for the silver lining in every dark cloud. This easygoing quality makes you one of the popular people at school or in your neighborhood. Even if you don't realize it, many people who meet you admire you, and like Hilary Duff, you are capable of starting fashion trends just by exercising your own individual style. The bad news is that Libras are a little spacey! Not in a Jessica Simpson way . . . it's just that Libras are big believers in the old saying that "a girl has a right to change her mind." Problem is, you like to change your mind over and over, and this can lead to problems. Also, you're so open and trusting that you can sometimes be a bit gullible.

Special Powers

A Libra is the most likely sign to feel psychic. This comes from the innate sense of understanding and a great ability to objectively analyze every situation. You're also likely to have artistic talents, even if you haven't discovered them yet. If you haven't, get going!

Things to Do

Try to be more decisive when problems arise and stick with your chosen path for longer than a day at a time. Make an effort to not butt in where

your admittedly strong sense of justice is not desired. And watch out for all that flirting you like to do—it's fun and games if the guy knows you, but if he doesn't, you might get a reputation as someone who's a little full of herself.

Your Future

Libra is the most desired sign of the zodiac for a reason! You are destined to have a relatively happy life because you are not a stressed-out type of person. Even big problems that come your way will be dealt with in a calm and intelligent manner. Future relationships will be characterized by your deep understanding of other people's POVs and your own acceptance of human limitations. You're not particularly jealous because you know you're all that and you feel strongly that if someone doesn't wanna be with you, it's their loss! Avoid going overboard with anything—partying, eating, vacationing—because while too much of a good thing is bad, too much of a bad thing is worse! You are likely to wind up in an intensely creative job, and you're predisposed to charity work, too.

Scorpio

The Scorpion (Water)
October 23–November 21
Personal Power Color: Maroon
Most Compatible Signs: Cancer and Pisces

The Big Picture

It's all about passion and determination for you. Whatever you set out to do, you finish, one way or another! People are sometimes amused by your single-minded drive, but they recognize that your loyalty and your honest nature are nothing to laugh at. Your enthusiasm is contagious and your depth of character and intellect make you someone who is consulted in matters serious and silly.

Special Powers

You have such a forceful nature, you may sometimes feel like life is one big lawn and you're the mower, leaving a path in your wake. Nothing gets you down and you're committed to never letting yourself down.

Things to Do

This sign is prone to jealousy, so when your date happens to speak to a rival or you think your steady boyfriend or girlfriend is cheating on you, take a step back and try to evaluate the situation. Consult others and also be sure to give the accused a chance to speak—it could just be your jealous nature reacting to innocent circumstances. If you're convinced, end it in a dignified way and avoid your tendency to be purposefully harsh.

Your Future

Scorpio, you are intense! You could make a brilliant surgeon or psychologist. Your self-control is such a skill it's almost a fault—make sure you don't allow yourself to become an iceberg of self-reliance. Other professions that would work for you include anything in nutrition and athletics (becoming a personal trainer would not be such a stretch . . . get it?). As a scientist, you may find yourself involved in discovering cures or reinventing procedures more than doing research or other more mundane but equally important aspects of your field. In work and in love, you will find total dedication—just like Hilary!

Sagittarius

The Archer (Fire)
November 22–December 21
Personal Power Color: Purple
Most Compatible Signs: Leo and Aries

The Big Picture

You're someone who believes that the biggest mistake anyone can make is having easy goals or none at all. You like to climb every mountain just because they're there and probably hold a record of some kind—maybe you were the fastest runner on the track team or were the last person standing at a dance marathon or won a chance to meet a star based on the most creative entry received in a national contest. You don't just dream big, you *do* big.

Special Powers

Your greatest gift is your enthusiasm, your uncanny ability to make even small tasks into worlds to conquer. Your sense of humor is legendary, and you can always be counted on to take any small setbacks with a grain of salt and with a hilarious, self-deprecating comment.

Things to Do

If you're going to focus on any self-improvement, it should be to buckle down and study more and improve your intellect. You're smart, to be sure, but you tend to hate studying and often skim reading assignments. (Other places to be!) You could also consider volunteering to do something selfless, such as supporting a charity that your idol Hilary Duff has endorsed.

Your Future

You really have a wide-open future. Your positive outlook on life will carry you far in any chosen field. You'd make a superb salesperson and would be a trusted and successful public relations expert for a celebrity of the stature of Hilary Duff. You're also great at determining your odds of success and failure, so would be good as a real-estate agent or stockbroker. Just be sure to avoid anything more risky, like gambling of any kind. For one thing, you might get too into the game. For another, Sagittarians are not good losers!

Capricorn

The Goat (Earth)
December 22–January 19
Personal Power Color: Royal blue
Most Compatible Signs: Taurus and Virgo

The Big Picture

Ambition is something that characterizes your every move. Not in a bad way! More likely, people have probably had definite ideas of where you were heading in life from before even *you* can remember. Like Hilary, you may have been honing your skills from an early age and winning credit for them from your peers. You don't take risks, you plot your best moves and then do everything according to plan—and come out on top every time! You're a perfectionist, baby—live it, love it.

Special Powers

Your ability to be self-disciplined is outstanding. You might be someone who is into vegetarianism or gymnastics (like Hilary), but whatever your passion is, you're good at it and unswerving in your drive to do it right. You're also a traditional person by nature, so you might be partial to the more classic way of doing whatever it is you do so well!

Things to Do
You gotta unwind! You're pretty high-strung thanks to being such a hard and dedicated worker, so relaxing on a vacation or by simply watching some brainless TV show every once in a while would work wonders on your stress level. Don't sweat the small stuff—you're doing great. And remember that it doesn't always have to be your way or the highway.

Your Future
Your Hilary-ish workaholic nature would make you a great candidate for law school or other professions that require copious amounts of preparation. You are likely to be a boss at any job you have (eventually) and are probably going to be the kind of person about which co-workers will say, "What did we ever do before she came to work here?" You're also funny enough to consider being a professional comedian, and are musically inclined, but you're more likely to be directly involved in management, either of people or of money.

Aquarius
The Water Bearer (Air)
January 20–February 18
Personal Power Color: Magenta
Most Compatible Signs: Gemini and Libra (Hil's sign!)

The Big Picture
Do people often tell you how smart you are? It's probably because you're so creative and so outgoing. You attract praise for your humanitarian pursuits as well as for your inventive streak. You don't sit back and participate in other people's projects—you design your own and you kick booty on them. You're friendly without being a social butterfly and you're really interested in making changes and in personal metamorphosis. Hmmm . . . where have we heard that word before?

Special Powers
A unique ability you have is that you can take in knowledge immediately! This could present itself in your ability to memorize lines from plays or for recitations, a knack for speed reading, or a great memory in general. You're a fast learner, may have skipped grades in school, and learn new languages as easy as *un, deux, trois.* Hilary has said she can now take in

whole scenes with just a glance at a script—you have this ability even more naturally than she does.

Things to Do

You may be someone who has been unfairly accused of being stuck up or rude simply because you tend to stand your ground and be outspoken. The latter are fine traits, but if you wanna win some popularity contests—or avoid fights with friends—you should exercise some tact and realize that little white social lies are okay if they're simply meant to keep everyone polite and happy. Develop your human side by watching emotional movies and reading deeply felt books, or by adopting a pet from your local humane society. Hilary's animals are rescue pets—make sure yours are, too!

Your Future

You're great in a group and, as you know, you love coming up with new ideas and gadgets. You might be destined to become a great inventor, or just a member of the family who can always be counted on to solve life's little dilemmas. You may find yourself drawn more to astronomy and other sciences far more than astrology (sorry, just skip this section!) and you're likely to win prizes for your work in whatever field you choose. Your ability to help those who are ill makes you a good candidate for medical school, especially psychiatry, but don't overlook other definitions of "technical" pursuits, including computer science and architecture.

Pisces

The Fish (Water)
February 19–March 20
Personal Power Color: Pink
Most Compatible Signs: Cancer and Scorpio

The Big Picture

You hate snobs more than anything else. You're very much a down-home type, someone who has great empathy for your fellow man. You think of haughty people as being downright antisocial and you have no patience for showboats. You take great pride in not being too proud! You're one of the most loving people your friends know, compassionate and philanthropic—but you detest getting attention for it. You don't lead, but you don't blindly follow. You're just yourself, and that is something many people constantly struggle to be.

Special Powers

You have incredible creativity that is reinforced by a loving sense of connectedness to humanity. You express yourself freely and your art is, first and foremost, for your own pleasure more than to achieve fame or money. Like Hilary Duff, you might be a poet or songwriter at the moment—and possibly will be one your whole life.

Things to Do

You should be sure to keep your intuition finely honed because Pisces can be great candidates to get punk'd. If you're punk'd by Ashton Kutcher, fine. But if you're punk'd by a con artist, not so fine! Don't trust too easily and don't let your guard down at bad times. Not everyone is as nice as you are!

Your Future

You would be a great travel writer thanks to your appreciation of escapism, but that same quality makes you a good candidate to be an artist. Some artists can be a little self-involved, but you would be more of a people's artist—perhaps a muralist or a writer of rock music like Hilary herself. You are a loner despite your loving nature, and will probably make your mark in a solitary position—as the owner of a small business, as a manager of a midsized business, or maybe even as a model. You're possibly psychically gifted (this is a trait most strongly possessed by Librans . . . but you already knew that!) and if not, you're very good at reading situations. Don't be shocked if you become famous for doing something you previously considered to be nothing more than a hobby!

Come Clean

The Hilary Duff Interviews!

The Early Daze Interview

January 16, 2003, Planet Hollywood Times Square, New York City

At this meeting, with mom, Susan, in tow, we lunched with a group at Planet Hollywood Times Square in Manhattan. Before I interviewed her, Hilary gamely posed in front of the restaurant's logo and even offered to pose in one of their T-shirts.

Hilary was still adjusting to the immense fame the *Lizzie McGuire* TV series had afforded her and described her life as being in a bit of a daze. Yet she was handling matters with her usual charm and poise!

And yes, she did eat the chicken crunch.

Hilary: *[To mother, Susan Duff] You can't listen, 'cause you'll make me nervous!*
Susan Duff: [Laughs]

Matthew: *Tell me your best date, worst date, last date, and first date!*
    Hilary: Best date . . . ahhh! Okay! Best date . . . oh, my God, I don't wanna answer this! [To Susan] First date was to a play, wasn't it? With Travis? . . .

Susan: *You went to Jim's Restaurant with the other Travis.*
    Hilary: No, that's not considered a date. First *and* worst I'm not gonna say his name because if he reads this he'll get upset. I was only like ten or something and we went together all dressed up with his family to see this *really scary* play. I don't even remember what it was, but it scared me so bad I just wanted to go home! I had a cell phone and I called my mom and I was like, "Mom! I'm so scared! I wanna come home!"

    Best date was probably . . . we went to Universal and to dinner and to a movie and bowling and it was totally fun . . . shut up, Mom!

    The last one . . . we just went to dinner and it was fun.

Matthew: *Do you have a best friend and do you have time for friends with your busy career?*
    Hilary: I think the term "best friend" is kinda mean. I know I have my really close friends, but I have my best friend from Houston which is Taylor, and I have my best friend from kindergarten, Lara, and my best friend in California, Tori. I think that

I have time for all of them and I always constantly talk to them on the phone, but it's hard, really hard.

Matthew: *What would you take with you to a desert island? Travis and Travis?*

Hilary: [Laughs] Yeah, I'd bring Travis and Travis. No, um, I'd take—

Susan: *I know: cell phone, lip gloss, and mascara.*

Hilary: I'd take my cell phone and my computer. And a phone jack connector to have someone come rescue me!

Matthew: *How was it working with Frankie Muniz, Aaron Carter, and Steven Tyler on* Lizzie McGuire?

Hilary: Mom, can you please start a conversation because I know what you're thinking and you're gonna answer my questions!

The coolest to work with was Steven Tyler because I love him. It was amazing and he was crazy, too, because he loves the show, he's a big fan. It was so funny! I was so flattered. I love Aerosmith and it was actually the last episode that we filmed.

It was cool working with Frankie, too. We're really good friends. It's nice to work with people that you know.

And then Aaron . . . it was fun. That's all I wanna say. It was cool because it was the very first guest spot we had on the show so it was lots of excitement.

Matthew: *Did you like working with your sister, Haylie, on* Lizzie McGuire?

Hilary: It was fun. We're always telling each other, "Do this here, do this here instead of that," so we're always giving each other tips and stuff, so it's fun. I also don't get to spend that much time with my sister, too, so it was fun working with her.

Matthew: *How do you feel knowing you're an idol?*

Hilary: It's weird because I know I've always idolized people, like, "Oh. I wanna be like them," like my sister or famous people or something. It's cool to know that people might do that to me. It's kinda weird at the same time, though, because I feel like a normal person.

Matthew: *How do you feel about people who are antifans, who say bad things about you out of jealousy?*

Hilary: At first I took it really personal. We really didn't have too many of that until Aaron Carter came on the show, and

then I was just like, "They don't even know me—why are they being so mean? Why do they not like me?" I understand if people don't like the show, but why say something bad about me? Change the frickin' channel. There's things on TV I don't like, but I don't say, "Oh, I hate this show!" Why don't we talk about positive things instead of negative? The girls that hate me because I dated Aaron Carter . . . I'm sorry, girls should be each other's best friend, and they're not, and that sucks.

Nothing offends me anymore—I think it just rolls off my back when I hear someone say something mean. I'm sorry they feel that way, but there's anger inside like . . . you haven't even given me a chance.

Matthew: *What's the best gift you've ever gotten?*

Hilary: It's so weird because I got asked that question the other day and it's not Christmas or my birthday. I think everyone gets whatever they want throughout the year. If you need a coat, you go buy a coat. If you want makeup, you go get makeup. That's how it is in my family. So it doesn't mean that much anymore to have a big, extravagant Christmas and stuff. I know that this year, I just wanted to get home. We got home two days before Christmas, so I was just happy to see my family. So that was my best gift.

Matthew: *Your fans love your hair. What do you do to it?*

Hilary: [Playfully] You mean my *natural* blond hair? [Laughs] I get it dyed once every three weeks . . . I get *highlights* every three weeks. I learn how to do stuff so much from watching people do my hair.

Matthew: *What acting did you do prior to* Lizzie McGuire?

Hilary: I did an episode of *Chicago Hope* and it was really kind of a dramatic role. I played a girl with a brain aneurysm. So it was really serious. And I did *Casper Meets Wendy*, which I was *such* a little kid in that, it's so *embarrassing* to see! And then I did a movie with Patricia Arquette called *Human Nature* and little commercials here and there and stuff like that.

Matthew: *Was it hard leaving Texas at an early age to move to Los Angeles?*

Hilary: It wasn't hard because I knew it was what I wanted to do. It's hard to be away from my dad, and I have another dog in Texas and my family and my home, but now I consider L.A. home because I love it so much. It just feels good to go back to Texas, even though I know I'm excited to leave and get back to L.A.

I didn't know anything was gonna happen, I just was gonna go out there and give it my best shot. I had no idea what to expect, either. And my mom—I owe everything to my mom and dad for supporting everything me and my sister wanted to do. When we came out to California, my mom bought all these books and read all these books and called all these people and worked so hard for us. So that was kinda hard, it was a big struggle with big sacrifices. But it wasn't hard to leave home because I loved it so much when I got there.

Matthew: *Were you sad filming the last episode of* Lizzie McGuire*?*

Hilary: It wasn't really a sad thing because Steven Tyler was on the show so it was really exciting and everyone was having a good time. We had a wrap party and it was weird because they knew I had to leave that Friday to go, but the night we wrapped, I flew to Vancouver to film *Agent Cody Banks* the next day, so it wasn't like I had a lot of time to think about it and be sad about it.

Now, looking back, I miss it. All those people became my family. I miss having a set schedule like that every single day and going in there and knowing what I'm doing.

Matthew: *Would you ever do another TV series?*

Hilary: That's what I'm trying to figure out right now. It locks me in there for three or four years playing the same character. That's what I like about movies, is I can do it and be done with it and never have to go back. Movies mean going out of town, so that makes things a little harder.

Matthew: *Would you ever do a clothing or makeup line?*

Hilary: I would love to. I don't think I'm ready for it right now—I'm too busy to think about stuff. But I love clothes and I love makeup and what sells me on makeup is good products that are cool but also the packaging. I could come up with some really cool packaging ideas!

Matthew: *Why did you decide to try singing?*

Hilary: I'll give you half the reason. I think that I never wanted to be a singer. . . . I'll give you the whole reason! When Aaron Carter came on *Lizzie McGuire,* he was a singer and he was act-

interview

ing and I thought, "I can do that! That looks fun. I can get up onstage and sing and dance around and have a good time."

So then I kind of really didn't tell anyone about it, I never took singing classes or anything like that. And then I saw my sister and she's a really good singer and she had a group for a while and I saw them rehearsing and singing and doing dance rehearsals and I was like, "Oh, my God! That looks like so much fun!" and I ran inside and told my mom, "Mom, I wanna be a singer! I wanna be a singer!" and I started going to voice class and I got a really good manager and one thing led to another and I was in a studio.

I like it! It's a good separation from acting. It's, like, *totally* different. For the album that's coming out in September or October, I'm gonna put a lot of time in it and really have the kind of music that I like and I feel is, like, related to something that's happened to me. I like the writers that I'm working with, too, because they know what I wanna sing about and kinda like my style. I think that I'm gonna write some, too.

Matthew: *How did you feel when* The Lizzie McGuire Soundtrack, *with your "I Can't Wait" on it, went gold?*

Hilary: I was excited! I think my mom was more excited. I had one song on it and there was tons of other really great artists on it, too. My mom told me and I was like, "Oh, my God! Cool!" and I was running in to do a scene for *Agent Cody Banks* and it was in Vancouver when I heard and I didn't have time to think about it until that night and I was like, "Oh, my God—I went gold!"

Matthew: *People have said you'll be the next Britney Spears. How does that feel?*

Hilary: I love Britney Spears, so of course I was flattered, I mean, Britney Spears is really cool, but . . . it was a shock. I don't think that I'm Britney Spears . . . she's huge! She's the biggest pop star ever. It was really cool and weird to hear. I didn't even see it. There was some interview on *Entertainment Tonight,* and my friend, who's obsessed with Britney Spears— she has her pictures all over her wall, her name's Tori—she called and said, "Do you know who they're calling the next Britney Spears?" and I was like, "What are you talking about???" It was pretty crazy.

Matthew: *Would you ever be in a girl group?*

Hilary: I don't know. I'd think about it. Sometimes, when I go onstage to perform, I get nervous, so I think it'd be easier to do with four other girls or something like that. Then I think that sometimes you don't always get along—so many groups break up! They all do. Even if they get along, they always want solo careers. It'd be fun, though, to dance around with them.

Matthew: *Will you be more into acting or singing in the future?*

Hilary: Acting was always the first thing, and it's what I knew I wanted to do since I was really little. I think if I had to choose, I'd choose acting, but I love both so I don't wanna pick an either/or right now. I think acting might last a little longer than singing!

interview

The *Metamorphosis* Interview

June 27, 2003

When I called Hilary at home for this exclusive talk, I was not surprised by her mom, Susan's, chitchat. Susan is one of the most down-home, friendly people you could ever meet. She goes out of her way to make you feel like a part of the family.

Susan also goes out of her way to maintain an atmosphere of normalcy for her family, something her comments illustrate in this, one of Hilary's longest and earliest one-on-one interviews about her solo CD *Metamorphosis*.

Matthew: *What's going on?*

Susan: We're scrambling as usual! We're in preproduction right now. . . . Hilary's trying to decide what she's gonna put on because she's gonna hook up with her friends and terrorize the neighborhood. [Laughs] They start filming *Cinderella* on Monday. [Hands phone to Hilary]

Hilary: Matthew! *How are you?*

Matthew: *Pretty good! First and foremost, tell me about your song "So Yesterday."*

Hilary: "So Yesterday" is a song that was written by The Matrix and, um, let's see, it was the last song I recorded for my album. It's funny because it's, like, the single. It's obviously about a relationship and we just shot the video for it the other day and it's funny because in the video my boyfriend and I get into a fight and it shows me spying on him. We see him going into the water to surf and I 'jack all his clothes. And then I take his shirt around and put it on all these crazy characters at the beach, like musclemen, like guys with all these tats, skater guys, this crazy lady with this big blond wig . . . and I start sending pictures to him.

I think it's a good message for girls because they think they have to have a boyfriend to be cool. The whole thing about it is that girls need to be independent. It shows it's easy to get over a boyfriend and after you wake up it's so yesterday.

Matthew: *Are you sneaky enough to do all that spying like the girl in the video?*

Hilary: It's funny because I'm really not like that at *all*. If a relationship is over for me, it's pretty much over. I'm not gonna go stalk the person. "So Yesterday" kinda shows that she's not even really doing it to get back to him—she just has a sense of humor. At the end, it shows him going to the mailbox and getting all these pictures and finally I leave this box with his clothes in it and a picture of me with the shirt on that says, "You're so yesterday."

Matthew: *So are you playing a character when you're doing a music video, kind of like acting?*
Hilary: Definitely. I wasn't only myself in the video because I don't think I'd do something like that. But it came out in the song. It was really fun and I had a good time. Making videos is definitely just like acting.

Matthew: *Did you know the guy who played your boyfriend in "So Yesterday"? Were you shy at your first meeting?*
Hilary: Oh, no! I had never met him before and there was, like, five guys and I picked him out of the five. Just by looking at the picture, he looked really cute. It was early in the morning and I was like, "Heyyyy, how are you? I'm Hilary, nice to meet you." I wasn't shy, but the first thing we did right in the morning, I came in and I had, like, no makeup on and looked so gross and we took a Polaroid together for the video and we had to be like we were boyfriend and girlfriend! That was a little creepy.

Matthew: *Tell me about some of the songs on your upcoming CD.*
Hilary: There's, let's see, a song called "Party Up" that I did with Meredith Brooks and it's really fun, a dance song, really rock, not too much pop in it, talking all about going out and having fun and stuff. I worked on another song called "The Math" by The Matrix, which is also about a relationship. I got to have so much say on the album, what the music sounded like and what I got to sing. Andre Recke—my manager—and my label have been so open to my opinions and stuff, which is cool, and I feel like I relate to all the songs.

Matthew: *Some first-time artists have no voice in their first records at all.*
Hilary: It was not like that at all with my album. I mean, definitely if they didn't think my opinion was good, they'd tell me! Other than that, it was really great.

Matthew: *Would you call your style of music "pop"?*
Hilary: I don't want to! I don't think that's a *bad* thing, but I just

think it's a little bit different than that. There's a bunch of different sounds on my album and there's definitely some songs that lead a little more to pop and some that are more pop/techno.

Matthew: *Are there any ballads?*
Hilary: Two or three.

Matthew: *What was the most challenging kind of song to sing for your album?*
Hilary: Let's see . . . I did this song called "Little Voices" [later retitled "Little Voice"] with this producer named Chico Bennett who worked on the song "Music" for Madonna and also "Bootylicious" for Destiny's Child. Then I worked with Kara DioGuardi. She wrote the song and it's so cool; it's talking about your conscience. It was really awesome, but it was really hard to sing because I don't sing really loud and I had to scream in this song. It still had to sound good, so it was a little bit of a challenge.

Matthew: *Why is* Metamorphosis *the ideal title for your CD?*
Hilary: Well, everyone keeps saying to me, like, "Uh-oh! What—are you gonna take your clothes off or something now?" and it's definitely *not* in that way. The metamorphosis, I've decided, is a metamorphosis for everybody else, a change. I think lots of people know me as my character Lizzie McGuire. This is more personal, it's a good way to get everybody to know more about *me*. There's actually a song on the album called "Metamorphosis." I was thinking, "Jeez, how can you make a song with that long of a word—metamorphosis—in it sound good and cool?" It's awesome, it's really rock and cool.

Matthew: *Were you in shock when you first realized that the "So Yesterday" video was on the TRL countdown?*
Hilary: Oh, my gosh, Matthew, you don't even understand. I was freaking out. I always watch *TRL* and it's just crazy. I didn't even know! My friend Alex, who lives right down the street from me, called me and he was like, "*Hilly Billy* . . . you're on *TRL*!" He was so excited. It's really cool and I'm definitely in great company.

Matthew: *Is Alex one of your good friends?*
Hilary: Yeah, I've known Alex for seven years. When I first came

out to California, he came out from Virginia and we lived in the same apartment complex. When I moved from the Oakwood Apartments where he was living, we moved down the street to [another complex], Alex moved there, too. Not because I moved there, just because it was a convenience. The [other complex is] on this street called Clybourn, and then I moved across the street to a house on Clybourn.

Alex is so cool about everything. He understands everything. Even when we're out, if it starts getting crazy, he'll take care of me. He's *sooo* cool. I love him.

Matthew: *Are you ready to tour and sing live?*
Hilary: [Little-girl voice] Yes! . . . I'm so nervous! I heard this story about Britney Spears the other day. I just worked with her choreographer for my video and I'm such a big fan of her, I love her, she's so cool. He was telling me about this concert that she did in Japan and it was raining on this runway that she was running on and she was running down waving to everyone and she just totally slipped in front of everyone. I would just start crying! I don't know what I would do.

Matthew: *Plus you have to get up in front of everyone and sing!*
Hilary: I am ready for that, actually. I'm ready to go.

Matthew: *Fans loved* The Lizzie McGuire Movie. *I especially loved Isabella!*
Hilary: Oh, you liked her? That was so much fun! I got to put that brown wig on.

Matthew: *The press went wild when you and Disney parted ways. What was the real scoop on that?*
Hilary: You know what, Matthew? The thing with that is, when *you* go see a movie, do *you* expect for there to be a sequel to every movie? No. There was never even ever put in for there to be a sequel. And with the TV show, you knew the TV show was over because all they do is sixty-five episodes, so the TV show was over a year and a half ago. They're making a big deal out of that, which is all Disney Channel ever picks up any of their shows for is sixty-five episodes. And then with the movie, there was never planned a sequel until after the movie came out and it was successful and they came and asked for a sequel and I was really busy, I had other stuff going on, and they wanted to do it right away, and I was like, "Well, you know, I can't because I've

got these other things planned." I'm totally open to it, and they just got really mad I guess. . . .

It's a big disappointment for me. I know the fans wanna see it. I'm open to anything.

Matthew: *You looked beautiful at the premiere of* The Lizzie McGuire Movie. *Did you plan your outfit forever?*

Hilary: No, my gosh, definitely not. It was so surreal. I was walking down the red carpet, like, "Oh, my God!" All these people were standing on the side of the street screaming and it was my name they were screaming. . . . It was crazy, but it was so cool. I was in shock almost.

I decided what to wear like fifteen minutes before I went—no joke. That day, I had to work all day on set for the movie *Cheaper by the Dozen.* We were working in Petaluma, which is out of town, and I flew in two hours before the premiere and figured out what I was wearing fifteen minutes before I went.

Matthew: *Aaron Carter gave you flowers . . . were you shocked he was there?*

Hilary: I didn't know he was gonna have flowers but it was really sweet.

Matthew: *Are you someone who's used to getting lots of flowers?*

Hilary: I just got some flowers in the mail the other day! But no, I'm not used to that.

Matthew: *Anything funny happen on the set of* Cheaper by the Dozen?

Hilary: It was never like *stunts* being pulled—everyone always wants good, funny stories like that—but everybody always joked around on set and had a great time and there were always kids running around so it was never a dull moment.

Matthew: *What's your* Cheaper by the Dozen *character like?*

Hilary: My character . . . her name is Lorraine and she's a fifteen-year-old girl who's really popular and her dad gets—if I'm making it seem like it's about me, it's not about me—but her dad gets a raise and we move out of town, which none of the kids want to do. The movie just shows the struggles of living in a family with twelve kids and the happy times and sad times and the hard times and the easy ones. It's just a really good, all-around story altogether and I think it's really hard to find new movies that the whole entire family can go and see, and that's what this really is.

interview

Matthew: *Aren't you almost filming* A Cinderella Story *by now?*

   Hilary: I start filming on Monday! I'm very excited. We've had rehearsals for the last couple of days and I'm really excited. I get to drive an old-fashioned Mustang.

Matthew: *How did you prepare for the starring role in* A Cinderella Story?

   Hilary: It's funny . . . I'm still doing it! We had lots of rehearsals. . . . I just wanted to make sure that there was absolutely no Lizzie in the character. She's a totally different girl. She has to deal with her horrible family life and her dad dying and she has to work all the time and she obviously doesn't get paid any attention to at school. There's lots of hard times and good times in the movie and everything ends up in her favor in the end, obviously.

Matthew: *Why do you think the Cinderella fairy tale is so powerful for girls?*

   Hilary: Every girl dreams of that, you know? Ever since you were little. Cinderella was definitely my favorite Disney movie of all time. It shows how strong she is in the end—she gets everything she wants.

Matthew: *What is Chad Michael Murray like in person?*

   Hilary: He's really cool. He's so down to earth and so nice and a really cool guy.

Matthew: *He's so much older than you! You're always paired with older guys in your movies!*

   Hilary: I know! Why do they do it to me? Chad's, like, twenty-one, he's a really cool guy and I like him a lot.

Matthew: *What was your* Vanity Fair *photo shoot like, the one all about teen stars?*

   Hilary: It was great. All of us, we were there together. Amanda and I were cool, she's such a cool girl and I love her so we had such a good time. And Mandy Moore and the Olsen twins, they're so down-to-earth, it was a really good shoot. Raven was there. . . . Nobody actually believed we were all there, but we were.

Matthew: *How do you like being involved in* Stuff by Hilary Duff?

   Hilary: I love it! I've got my clothing line. There's so much cool stuff that I get to do—pick out colors and fabrics and threads and material and the cuts of the clothes. It's just a cool process. Oh, my gosh, insane amounts of things. I wake up every single day and I don't have one style that I stick to. I feel inspired every single day by different moods or whatever and it's really cool that I get to make that and hopefully young girls will wear it.

I had so many ideas when we got started and I pulled everybody into my closet and I was like, "This is what I love and this is what I hate." I never throw clothes away because I always feel like I can cut 'em up or do something and fix 'em into a different way. I have this big box of stuff that I pulled out and we played. It was fun.

Matthew: *You always look perfect. Do you ever dress slobby?*

Hilary: Oh, my gosh—all the time! In my neighborhood, there's this place called Bob's Big Boy and we always go up there in our pajamas on Sunday morning.

Matthew: *How do you like your room?*

Hilary: I love my room! In four days I went from New Jersey, New York, Miami, Tampa, Fort Lauderdale, Seattle, Portland, Denver, and then Sacramento. It was insanely crazy. I hate hotel rooms and I totally respect my room now. I have so much jewelry that I filled up a whole corkboard with jewelry so it adds lots of color, and I have red walls and cheetah carpet and my room's really fun, but we're getting ready to redecorate it with pretty, soft pinks and greens.

Matthew: *Do you think people in the business sometimes forget you're as young as you are?*

Hilary: I do sometimes! But not in a bad way. I think me being in the business and used to being around people in the business, sometimes people don't know how to treat a fifteen-year-old girl and they treat me like an adult—which is fine, it's cool, I feel like I'm mature enough to have a conversation with adults all the time. I like for people to talk to me like that. I wouldn't like it if they talked to me like a kid.

Matthew: *Do people ever treat you like a total baby?*

Hilary: Not too bad. I've been so lucky to come across people who've been so friendly and nice and cool.

Matthew: *You've done so much already—what is left for you to dream about?*

Hilary: Oh, my gosh, Matthew—that's a big question. I haven't thought about that too much yet because I don't wanna freak myself out. I wanna say I love my job, I love working and all the responsibilities that come with that, too, and hopefully I'll have a really successful album and can continue making albums and the same with my clothing line and everything. I wanna go to college. I do care about school . . . and I'm not gonna think past that point.

You know what I love? I love that I wake up in the morning and I have no idea what's planned for me that day. It's not like the same old thing over and over and over again.

I pretty much wait until that day because I don't wanna get all crazy planning it out and stuff!

interview

The Superstar Interview

September 1, 2003, Hyatt Regency Kauai Resort and Spa, Kauai, Hawaii

In 2003, I interviewed Hilary after dark on the beach of Kauai on the expansive grounds of the Kauai Hilton. We were all staying there as she filmed her TV birthday special for The WB and when I finally got a hold of the blond dynamo, she had just been given a birthday *car* by her parents as the final scene of the special.

A hurricane had blown dangerously close to the area and we were feeling the breeze and hearing the riled-up waves a few yards from us as we huddled together on folding chairs for this in-depth chat.

Right after we finished, Hilary spotted some surfer dudes who had snuck up and were hovering nearby in hopes of getting autographs. I got my interview and they got their autographs!

Matthew: *How do you feel knowing your album* Metamorphosis *went to number 2 in its first week, selling over 200,000 copies? Then hit number one the following week?*

Hilary: It's seriously crazy—I cannot believe it. [Nearby surfer boy shouts: "You're cute!"] Thank you! [Passing fan says: "Happy birthday!"] Thank you! [Back to Matthew] It's amazing. I seriously cannot believe it's me and that there's so many fans out there that like the music and they bought my CD. It's really, really exciting and so amazing. There's not even words to describe it—it's such a great shock. I was really nervous when it first came out because I was like, "Oh, my gosh, the album's *really* coming out!" and it was so scary, then it came out and I saw the reaction and the CD was selling out everywhere so I was like, "Oh, my gosh, this is so cool!" So everything worked out good.

Matthew: *The album is great!*

Hilary: Thank you! Thanks! I have people coming up to me and saying, "We love it!" and "We can't believe how much it sounds older and it sounds great." I think the music really means something and doesn't talk down to younger fans.

Matthew: *How was your first-ever performance?*

Hilary: I was nervous! I was like, "Oh, my God, what if I do horrible?" but the crowd, they helped me out so much. They were so excited and they had so much energy, which really helped me, too.

Matthew: *You didn't look nervous at all.*

Hilary: I didn't? That's good—then I put on a good front!

Matthew: *Did you rehearse a lot?*

Hilary: We'd been rehearsing a little bit but not too much because I had been working every single day on *A Cinderella Story,* and then after work I'd go work an hour and a half with the band. So, not *too much* dance rehearsal or anything like that.

Matthew: *Tell us about your Hawaiian experience!*

Hilary: Oh—my—*God!* It's been incredible, like, I don't wanna leave. I can't believe all my friends surprised me here. I thought it was just gonna be a family vacation—and that would be fun, too—but this is, like, even better.

When we first got here, we went up to the room and the room is, like, so incredible—it's so beautiful!—and the hotel and the beaches and all the lagoons and the pools. . . . And then we got to do so many cool things, like I went scuba diving and we learned how to surf. We went on this huge boat adventure where we went through all these caves and stuff—I've never seen anything like it before.

Matthew: *Do you think you and your friends will cherish the experience?*

Hilary: Words can't describe it. We're gonna all remember this forever.

Matthew: *How did you like your scrapbook they made for you?*

Hilary: It was so beautiful! I was like, "Oh, my gosh—I can't believe they all made it for me!" It was really great.

Matthew: *Were you expecting all the surprises on your trip?*

Hilary: Not a *car!* But it was really cool. And then even the scrapbook—it kinda went day by day with all the things that we've done and all the behind-the-scenes moments. That was so fun. And no, I didn't expect a car; no, I didn't expect my friends to be here; I didn't expect Simple Plan to be here—it was so exciting. They were really nice!

Matthew: *How was your 2003 MTV Video Music Awards experience?*

Hilary: It was awesome. I had a great time. I got to see so many people that I love and it was fun being onstage and I got to present with Jason Biggs—he was really cool—and I got to see the whole Britney/Madonna/Christina thing, which was really cool. I was a little shocked, actually, but I guess that's what it's all about—the shock factor.

Matthew: *Did you go out to all the parties?*

Hilary: I *didn't* go out and party because I had to get up at four in the morning to be at the airport by six to fly to Hawaii—no time. But I had a great time, like, Fred Durst came up to me and I was like, "I have a confession to make—I love you, you're awesome! My sister and I jam out to you in the car all the time!" And there were so many sweet people sitting next to us, like Nelly.

Matthew: *Britney Spears recently sang your praises—how does that make you feel?*

Hilary: It makes me feel, like, really amazing and gives me a little bit of confidence because the whole singing thing is very new to me, and Britney Spears is such an idol of mine. I think she is a fantastic performer, she's multitalented, she's absolutely beautiful and I think a lot of people give her flak for some of the things she does, catching her partying or—how old is she? Twenty-one?—you know what I mean? *Everybody* does that at that age and she just happens to be in the spotlight getting caught doing it all. She has done so much for everybody and there's so many little girls that look up to her. And even about the way she dresses and stuff—if she's comfortable, more power to her. I think she rocks. I think she's awesome and she's so talented.

Matthew: *Are you psyched to take your show on the road . . . on tour?*

Hilary: I'm nervous to go overseas just 'cause I'm not a good flyer, but I can't wait to see the girls over there. We're gonna go to Australia and Japan and Germany and so many cool places, so it's exciting. And I love my band and I love traveling with them.

Matthew: *They're so nice!*

Hilary: Aren't they nice? All of them. And so talented. They're like, "Oh, our little rock star, she's getting comfortable onstage!" They're so nice and very encouraging.

Matthew: *You're not a good flyer. . . but you fly all the time!*

    Hilary: I *do* fly all the time. I try to make myself go to sleep or watch movies and stuff. Actually, it sounds corny, but I pray all the time on flights! I'm totally, like, "Angel! Please help me get through this flight!" You know what I mean? You just have to calm yourself down. But, like, the second turbulence starts going, I'm like [pants fearfully]—I can't believe it, I freak out!

Matthew: *When you hear* Metamorphosis *playing, does it feel real? Does it feel like you?*

    Hilary: It's so weird because you hear Britney Spears and Nelly and it seems so big and then to hear *my* songs up next to them it just doesn't seem normal, it seems crazy. I'm such a normal person, I'm from Texas. . . . All the good stuff happening to me just doesn't seem real.

Matthew: *What is your fave song of all your songs?*

    Hilary: I don't have one. Seriously, I listened to my album the other day and I was like, "You know what? I'm really proud of this. I love all the songs on the album and I really relate to them." There's a couple that I really love to perform—I love to perform "Little Voice," "Party Up," "Metamorphosis."

Matthew: *No plans for TV or more movies just yet?*

    Hilary: I never wanna quit either one, but right now I wanna focus on music—I had a really good time up on that stage! It was cool because I got to interact with the audience.

Matthew: *Our time is running out! So think fast—what's a secret no one knows about you?*

    Hilary: I don't know how to answer that . . . there's not too much that I hide. A secret . . . I do *not* eat eggs. I call it prelife, it's so nasty. I don't like they way they look, I don't like the way they smell, I don't like the noise they make in your mouth or when you cut them. Yuck—can't stand that!

Matthew: *Oh, Hilary—the scandal of it all!*

    Hilary: [Laughs, runs to sign autographs in the dark]

Hilary Duff from A to Z

Your Own Duff-cyclopedia

For casual fans and crazy diehards, this is *the* list of odds and ends that make up the Hilary story!

American Dreams

The Duff sisters appeared as the Shangri-Las in an episode of this heart-warming NBC show, set around *American Bandstand* in the '60s.

Band

Hilary's band consists of sexy guitarist Jason "Hook," nimble-fingered Loren Gold on the piano/keyboards, the mesmerizing Shauney Baby on the drums, and bewitching backing singers Sibucao (identical triplets Abbey, Baili, and Rachel Sibucao). Hilary is fiercely loyal toward her band and vice versa. Trusty Ty Stevens is her musical director and also a guitarist.

Never "board" with keyboardist Loren!

Rockin' on with Jason!

That's Shauney Baby, baby!

The lovely Sibucao Sisters!

123

Barrymore, Drew
The star of *Ever After: A Cinderella Story* was Hilary's number one choice to guest star on *Lizzie McGuire*. She didn't get her wish, but she did wind up filming a movie called *A Cinderella Story*! Other actresses Hilary has cited as ideal costars have included Susan Sarandon, Julia Roberts, and Britney Spears. She has professed a hope that she'll one day work with Sandra Bullock, too, because "she's funny, pretty, and a great actress!"

Beckham, David
Mr. Posh Spice, England's number one athlete, is one of Hilary's most consistently cited celebrity crushes. By 2004, she was conceding to Australia's *New Weekly* that "he's too old for me and he's married!"

Birthday
Hilary was born September 28, 1987.

Blender
Hilary posed for this music mag's front cover and for an interior spread in the October 2004 issue. While many other female stars pose in next to nothing, Hilary kept it tasteful, showing no more than any normal girl would walking down the street in the summer. The most provocative aspect of this shoot was the decision to pose in a Mickey Mouse T-shirt . . . take *that*, Disney!

Hilary's steadfast modesty, even as her peers flaunt their bodies, is one reason why her fans respect her. Big sis Haylie sees it like this: "That's a great thing about my sister—she hasn't moved into the crop-top, showing-all-her-skin-off clothes." Haylie thinks this is a selling point when it comes to Hil's Stuff by Hilary Duff brand. "With her clothing line, she's stressing to girls, 'You can be sexy and you can be hot and you can dress older than your age—but you don't have to take off all your clothes to do it.'" Right on, sister! (Literally.)

Bob's Big Boy
One of Hil's fave places to hang out and also to have breakfast with friends. But this was also the site of a particularly strange fan encounter in 2001, when *Lizzie McGuire* was first making Hilary famous. Hilary was there with Haylie and Haylie's friends and she excused herself to go to the bathroom. A pack of four girls immediately followed her and, as Hilary recalled it, had their ears pressed up to the stall! Haylie had noticed the girls and came to Hilary's rescue, calling the overzealous fans "sick!"

Hilary's Seventeenth Birthday Bash!

Hilary enjoyed her best birthday ever, surrounded by friends and family at home in Los Angeles!

A Cinderella Story costar Dan Byrd and big sis, Haylie, help Hil tally up all her birthday loot!

Hilary beams with her Louis Vuitton haul!

Who wants a cell phone when you can have this adorable Hello Kitty phone instead!

The Duff ladies have their cake and eat it, too!

Hilary prepares to blow out the candles on her birthday sushi!

Boys

Being a famous hottie, Hilary finds that guys sometimes are too intimidated to approach her—even when it would be welcome! When *Lizzie McGuire* was becoming a tween hot topic, she related this story: "This one boy was just staring at me while I was at the mall with my mom. It was like right after work—this boy was *hot!* He was sitting there with some of his friends and he was looking and I was thinking, 'Please come over here, please come over here!' But he never did! My mom was like, 'Hilary, go over and talk to him.' And I said, 'Mom! What's wrong with you? No!'"

In her movies, she's often paired up with older leading men, from Yani Gellman to Chad Michael Murray to Oliver James. It's not always Hilary's choice—blame the producers! "I think there's definitely a shortage of cute fourteen- and fifteen-year-old guys . . . at least from what I've seen," Hilary says. "Bring 'em on!" But she isn't into pretty boys, having said, "I don't like guys that look like they spend more time in front of the mirror than I do!"

Dating can be hard as a superstar. She told *New Weekly* that "it gets really hard" forming committed relationships. She denied having a type, and said, "I'm very open-minded about the way people look or whatever. I like someone very funny. I like to laugh a lot and have a good time. I definitely don't like lazy people!" Guys, consider yourself tipped off!

Brunette

Hilary considered dying her hair dark in 2004, but decided against it when she figured she'd tire of it but be unable to go blond again without damaging it. In this writer's humble opinion, Hilary made a ravishing brunette as Isabella in *The Lizzie McGuire Movie.*

Bush, Jenna

The First Daughter was Hilary's camp counselor back in Texas. "She was really sweet. I loved her!" Hilary enthused to *Time* magazine.

Car

Hil's dream car in 2002 was a Mercedes. By 2003, she was fantasizing about a hot pink Hummer, a BMW, or an SUV. She currently drives a Range Rover.

Carter, Aaron

Most of Hilary's fans know that Aaron and Hilary dated, and that he caused their relationship to end by dating other girls.

"Aaron Carter was my first love," she told *CosmoGirl!*—and he beeped her on the other line during that magazine's first interview with her!

Back in the spring of 2001, Hilary was already dealing with some backlash for reportedly dating Aaron. She told reporter Rana Meyer, "When he's not around all the press people and everyone else, he's a totally different guy and he's so cute." He even gave her roses for Valentine's Day that year, though she did not get to see his Las Vegas concert stop (as sis Haylie and her girl group Trilogy did) because of her *Cadet Kelly* shooting schedule.

Hilary apparently met Aaron at his December 2000 birthday party and then later when he was asked to guest star on *Lizzie McGuire*. When they dated (on and off, for about a year and a half), it was mostly to dinner and the movies and once to Hilary's director's Super Bowl party. Originally, Aaron was slated to film a second *Lizzie McGuire* episode, which Hilary says was kind of like *Notting Hill*—but it never happened. Aaron later showed up at the L.A. premiere of *The Lizzie McGuire Movie* with flowers for Hilary, who was surprised and touched by the gesture.

It did not lead to a lasting reunion.

CBS

In early 2004, it was announced that Hilary had a development deal with CBS for a *Family Ties*–esque sitcom. But like her stalled talks with The WB and ABC for series, the call of movies and CDs threw up roadblocks. Will Hilary do another TV series one day? Keep your fingers crossed!

Cheating

Hilary has confessed to cheating on spelling in the second grade by writing words in her desk. She got caught and it bothered her so much she never cheated again.

Chicken crunch

Planet Hollywood fried appetizer that Hilary loves. Despite being in shape, Hilary does love to eat!

Chicken Soup for the Soul

Hilary adores this series of books, which she lists among her favorites.

Cinderella

This 1950 animated masterpiece is Hilary's favorite Disney movie of all time. No wonder she was so eager to star in *A Cinderella Story*, an updated version of the classic tale!

Cine-Manga

Published by TokyoPop, Inc., this series of illustrated novelizations of popular TV series and movies has not overlooked the appeal of *Lizzie McGuire*! There are already a dozen *Lizzie* titles in print with more on the way. Each volume uses color images from episodes along with word balloons to help fans carry around their favorite show for a quick flip-through at any time!

College

When you're rich and famous, is there a need to go to college? Yes! College is a great way to get grounded, get an education, and find yourself, not *only* the place you go in hopes of earning more money later on. Hilary has repeatedly stated that she would like to attend college when the time is right. "I definitely want to go to college. It's so far down the line, but I definitely care about school," she said firmly around the time she was promoting *Cadet Kelly*, set in a military school. "So many kids say they hate school, and actually last year I feel like I didn't learn that much because I didn't pay attention. I was kind of behind. But now I'm in the eighth grade and this year I love it. I just realized I had to crack down . . . although I *do* hate homework!"

Color Me Mine

Instead of partying, Hilary says she prefers going to this make-your-own-pottery place with Haylie. Check it out at colormemine.com. You can't make this stuff up!

Cooking

Hilary doesn't have the time or patience to cook elaborately, but she told *Rolling Stone* that she cooks on her George Foreman Grill. "All of my friends are obsessed with my grilled cheese sandwiches. They're messy looking but taste so good."

Cover

Hilary's first magazine cover was the April 2002 issue of *Popstar!* magazine.

Hilary Duff

Crazy

As hard as it is to believe, this is the one word Hilary said her best friend would use to describe her, circa 2001.

Crystal Light

In 2002, Hilary told an interviewer this low-cal drink was always in her fridge. Oh, and dill pickles!

Dates

Unless she's seriously dating a boy, Hilary has said she prefers to avoid "one-on-one dates." Instead, she favors group gatherings for sushi or to an underage club.

Dogs

Little Dog Duff was Hilary's most famous pet, a pooch she referred to as her "total princess." Sadly, the fox terrier/Chihuahua mix passed away in 2004, just before the doggie line named for her hit the shelves. Other dogs Hilary's had are a border collie (Remington, back home in Houston) and a pit bull/boxer mix in Los Angeles. Currently, Hilary and Haylie own the adorable Macy and Bentley and a Chihuahua named Chiquita adopted from a Much Love Animal Rescue benefit at Luxepets in Los Angeles.

Doll

Playmates offers a series of Hilary Duff fashion dolls, including Rock Star, Movie Star, and TV Star, and there are of course many Lizzie dolls out there—some are even legitimately licensed. Hilary said in 2004, "It's a little unnerving seeing yourself as a doll . . . but lots of fun!"

Dorkerella

Kate Sanders calls Lizzie McGuire this—oh so affectionately—in *The Lizzie McGuire Movie.*

Dr Pepper

Red Bull may be the "in" drink for energy-challenged teens, but Hilary often prefers to sip on this soft drink at her photo shoots! "I drink it all the time—it's on all my sets!" she told *USA Today.*

Durst, Fred

The unpredictable front man of Limp Bizkit has had run-ins with other divas, notably Christina Aguilera and Britney Spears. But he apparently gives Hilary her props and shows no signs of bad-mouthing her! At The 2003 MTV Video Music Awards, Fred approached Hil and said, "Hilary, you're such a cool girl! I love everything you're doing. Keep a straight head—you rock!" Believe me, when *Fred Durst* says you rock, *you rock!*

Eggs

Hilary despises this food and avoids them like the plague! "I'll eat anything except for eggs!" she says.

Embarrassing moments

Lizzie has had way more than Hilary has, but the girl who can pratfall gracefully has had her share of red-faced moments. One of her worst was in 2001. As she told *Popstar!* magazine: "My boyfriend over the summer, Brandon, they were moving in to a different house in the neighborhood. They were coming to pick me up and I was going swimming over at his house. I was sitting on someone's lap because there was no other room in the car and I had my hair up in one of those clips. They close the door and my hair is caught in the door. I was so embarrassed to say anything. So now they call me Blondie!" Ouch.

Eminem

You might expect a wholesome artist like Hilary to be anti-Eminem, but she loves his work and has called him a "musical genius." She's said, "Even though I don't necessarily agree with lots of things he says, because he says some awful things about women and drugs and stuff like that . . . his music is so catchy you just want to sing along."

Fans

Hilary loves her fans and even dedicated her *Hilary Duff* CD to them. She always makes time for autographs and is genetically predisposed to being polite and gracious. Occasionally, she has wacky fan encounters. One of the weirdest was when she was at a department store with her sister and mom. A little girl was shadowing her and finally the little girl's mom asked Hilary if she was the girl from *Lizzie McGuire.* This caused the shy fan to freak out and shove and pull her mom's hair, which earned her a sharp rebuke. They fought until the little girl darted off, at which time the mom turned to a speechless Hilary Duff and said, "Thanks a lot! You have just embarrassed my daughter!" If you see Hilary in real life . . . don't do this.

Fender bender

"I don't even get to have a cool story or anything like that," Hilary told *J-14* magazine in its December 2004 issue of her one and only driving disaster. She scratched her Range Rover pulling into her garage!

Flying

Hilary's not a fan of what planes do, but she's improved since 2002, when she fearfully told reporters prior to her first-ever European trip, "I'm a freaky flier!"

Fortune

As in, "Hilary's worth a . . ." According to conservative estimates, she is already worth close to $25 million and stands to gain exponentially from her Stuff by Hilary Duff line, album royalties, concert tours, and other endeavors.

Friends

Hilary has a tight circle of friends. Her closest pals, all of whom accompanied her to Hawaii for *Hilary Duff's Island Birthday Bash*, are [front row L–R] Taylor Hoover, Marco Milani, [back row L–R] Britney Stone, Eliana Reyes, and Alex Stamm.

GameBoy

Disney Interactive has released two *Lizzie McGuire*–themed games for this system: *Lizzie McGuire: On the Go* and *Lizzie McGuire 2: Lizzie's Diaries*.

"Girl Can Rock"

Hilary's rockiest song appeared on overseas pressings of her *Metamorphosis* CD and was one of the highlights of her WB special *Hilary Duff's Island Birthday Bash* in September 2003. The song is also found on a special version of *Metamorphosis* in the United States that's only available in Target.

Good Charlotte

Though the tabloids have linked Hilary with Good Charlotte's front man, Joel Madden, Hilary herself has denied they're involved. Her former spokeswoman in 2004 said, "They're just friends. She might have met Good Charlotte at a radio show, but either way, she's friends with the whole band." She's a huge fan of their music, and has been spotted with a pink MADE brass knuckles necklace. "I think my 'boyfriend' is my work and my car," Hilary has joked.

Good luck

Hilary believes in luck and has been known to carry pictures and notes from people she loves in her wallet. She also obsessively hoards every fortune-cookie slip she finds.

Good Morning America

In 2004, more than seven thousand people swarmed Manhattan's Bryant Park to see and hear Hilary and Haylie Duff perform.

Gossip

Hilary hates the stuff. While everyone in Hollywood is the subject of rumors or happily spreading them, Hilary avoids gossipy conversations whenever she can.

Got Milk?

Hilary's ad for the Milk Advisory Board was photographed by David LaChapelle and showed her with shopping bags under the phrase, "Shop and not drop."

Hollywood Squares

Hilary has appeared on the TV game show twice, once with TV mom, Hallie Todd, and once with real-life sis, Haylie.

Horses

Along with dogs, horses are Hilary's fave animal. Her family bought two Shetland ponies, Cinnamon and Sugar, at their church auction and kept them on their Bastrop ranch, where they also owned a Welsh pony named Lady. "Horses have always been special to me," Hil told *Cowboys & Indians* magazine.

Ice cream

As a special treat and to say thank you to the cast and crew of *A Cinderella Story*, Susan Duff had her favorite ice cream flown in from Texas and served on set the final day of filming in Los Angeles.

Karaoke

If you wanna sing along to Hilary Duff and other fun pop, try *Disney's Karaoke Series: Lizzie McGuire*—you can try your hand (and more importantly, your voice!) at "I Can't Wait," "Why Not," and "What Dreams Are Made Of"!

Lamberg, Adam

This actor played Gordo in the *Lizzie McGuire* series and in *The Lizzie McGuire Movie*. Born on September 14, 1984, Adam is now attending college at UC Berkeley in California, where he reports he is not often recognized (it might be because he's grown his hair so long!). Fans always hoped Lizzie and Gordo would hook up at the end of the series, but the closest they came was a kiss at the end of the film version. In real life, the two are good friends. In 2002, Hilary considered coproducing a movie with Adam, who has said, "Hilary's like a little sister to me!"

Lavigne, Avril

It all started when Hilary was told a story about Avril that made it seem like Avril was dissing her own fans. Hilary deplored this and Avril struck back, calling Hilary a "goody-goody," the ultimate slam in this day and age. Hilary, realizing she was unwittingly caught in a media-made cat-fight, backpedaled and apologized. "I really didn't mean to offend Avril," she told *Blender* magazine in 2004, "but when I did, she hit back by calling me a goody-goody, and said that I'm all smiles. Okay, I guess I'm fine with that. I am a happy person, and I do smile a lot. But just because I don't go out and party like other young Hollywood types and stay out until five o'clock in the morning doesn't necessarily mean I'm a goody-goody, does it?" No, it just means you won't be burned out before age twenty-one.

Hilary has gone on to say that she doesn't care if Avril despises her and her image, she is still a big fan of Avril's work and even owns both of her CDs!

"Little Voice"

This track from *Metamorphosis* is all about Hilary having a conversation with her conscience. It's also the song Hilary has said was the hardest for her to sing due to the louder parts.

Los Cabos

Immediately before her whirlwind 2004 tour of Japan and Australia, Hilary and Haylie spent about five days off in this red-hot resort town in Mexico. Just how hot is red hot? Gwyneth Paltrow and Chris Martin spent their honeymoon here and Brad Pitt and Jennifer Aniston used to vacation in the vicinity. Rumor has it Hilary went cliff diving, deep-sea diving, and reeled in a fifty-pound mahimahi that was cooked and served to her group that evening.

Hil and Hay have also vacationed on Catalina, a trip they made in December of 2003. They love playing together almost as much as they love working together!

Loves

Hilary's list of things she loves would be too long to include in this book. But she memorably once summed it up as laughing, eating, shopping, and trying new things!

Mandela, Nelson

The great South African dignitary who survived decades in prison as an apartheid opponent is one of Hilary's biggest heroes. "Every kid should know who Nelson Mandela is," she's said, "and they should do reports on him because he's such an amazing human being. He's truly a hero. He's awesome." Hilary met him in the summer of 2002 when she was able to attend a Special Session on Children at the United Nations. She confessed to being "nervous!" beforehand, but it was one of the many highlights of her life.

Masterson, Jordan "Jordy"

The younger brother of Danny (*That '70s Show*) and Chris (*Malcolm in the Middle*), Jordy was a datemate of Hilary's for a couple of months in 2004. She confirmed her breakup in *Popstar!*, where she spilled, "We broke up . . . and it's just better. I work so much." She went on to make a very empowering statement, one all young girls need to take to heart! "I think girls . . . feel like they're not cool unless they have a boyfriend or they don't feel comfortable or happy with themselves—that's not true! You gotta be independent! You gotta show the power!"

"The Math"

This track from Hilary's *Metamorphosis* CD happens to be her father's favorite!

Matrix, The

This songwriting and production team is made up of Lauren Christy, Graham Edwards, and Scott Spock. They came to international prominence working with Avril Lavigne to craft the sound behind her *Let Go* album and even won a Grammy for Song of the Year for their collaboration with the crabby Canadian on "I'm With You." Hilary's smash hit "So Yesterday," the attitude-packed "The Math," and the aching ballad "Where Did I Go Right?" were all produced and written by this gifted trio. Did you know The Matrix is also a band? Along with added members A.K.A. and Katy Perry, The Matrix will release a debut album on Columbia later this year. Other artists who've been "reloaded" by The Matrix include Britney Spears, Christina Aguilera, Busted, Liz Phair, Jason Mraz, David Bowie, and Shakira.

Monkeys

Monkeys is the imaginary password Oliver James's character, Jay Corgan, says Hilary's character Terri Fletcher must utter in order to enter her dorm the first night she arrives in Los Angeles in a scene from the movie *Raise Your Voice*.

Most Wanted Tour

Hilary's summer 2004 concert tour, in which she rocked audiences worldwide, firmly established her as a premier live rock act.

Movies

Hilary's fave movie changes almost every time I ask her, but among the movies she seems most drawn to are *Chicago, Drop Dead Gorgeous, Romy and Michelle's High School Reunion, Finding Nemo, Bruce Almighty, Charlie's Angels,* and *How to Lose a Guy in 10 Days*. She is not a fan of heavy, sad movies, but she does like the more dramatic *I Am Sam*.

GIRL CAN ROCK
LITTLE VOICE
TALK
COME CLEAN
TALK
SO YESTERDAY
ANYWHERE
METAMORPHOSIS
TALK
SWEET SIXTEEN
WHERE DID I GO
LOVE JUST IS
TALK
WHY NOT
DO THE MATH
WORKING IT OUT
TALK
PARTY UP
GOODBYE
****
MY GENERATION

Murray, Chad Michael

Hilary's costar in the Warner Bros. summer 2004 film *A Cinderella Story* is none other than this *One Tree Hill* hottie. Chad and Hilary were rumored to be dating when they appeared at The WB's press tour party and The Teen Choice Awards together, but Hilary stomped out those rumors quickly. "He's way too old for me!" she said. Chad spent lots of time with the Duffs during the filming of *A Cinderella Story,* and loved having a family to bond with since his own was so far away, back in Buffalo, New York.

Music

Hilary's musical tastes are, like any teenage girl's, ever changing. In early interviews, she was taken with *NSYNC, Britney Spears, and BBMak (back in the day, she said she was jealous when they appeared on *Even Stevens*). More recently, she has cited classic rock like the Eagles, Bob Dylan, Santana, and Janis Joplin as faves. Contemporary favorites include Boomkat, Black Eyed Peas, Matchbox 20, Eminem, Missy Elliott, Linkin Park, Justin Timberlake, Good Charlotte, Michelle Branch, and Vanessa Carlton.

"My Generation"

Hilary covered this The Who classic in 2004 during her *Most Wanted* Tour, but she did so at the displeasure of many rock purists—they were upset that she sang "I hope I *don't* die before I get old" instead of the original, more rebellious lyric. Hilary's response to the haters? Lighten up, it's just a song.

New York Yankees

Hil's fave major-league baseball team! She even appeared on several episodes of *Kids on Deck* on the Yankees's YES Network in the New York City area. In the popular skits, she talked baseball to her fellow teens and tweens. "I just talk about different baseball issues," Hilary said at the time. "It's coming from the perspective of someone who's just learning about baseball and making all these discoveries about it. For example, did you ever notice that umpires and parents have similar jobs?"

Pink

This is one of Hilary's very favorite colors . . . but she also confesses her fave color sometimes changes week by week! In 2004, she dyed her hair pink. "I just decided to dye it pink," she told the venerable *Tiger Beat* magazine. "I wanted to do something different."

Pinkston, Ryan

The hilarious star of *Punk'd* and FOX's *Quintuplets* had a long-term crush on Miss Hilary! In 2003, he confessed, "Hilary is on top of the world right now. Not only can she act but she has a great singing voice, too. We will be seeing her around for a long time! I wish her the best of everything." He eventually met her and was mortified when a friend of his swiped her cell phone number and made some immature calls to her line. Oops. Another Pinkston connection? It turns out that Ashton Kutcher had enlisted Hilary Duff to punk Ryan . . . but plans fell through. Lucky for Ryan!

Plastic surgery

Every famous girl, sooner or later, gets accused of having work done, whether it's true (Keira Knightley admitted fluffing her upper lip) or false. Hilary told *Life Story* in 2004 that the most outrageous rumor she's heard about herself involved her getting a boob job—at age sixteen! "Girls grow up, and just because you're not the same size that you were when you were ten doesn't mean that you got something done."

Premios Oyo

In 2004, Hilary was nominated as Best New Anglo Artist at this Mexican version of the Grammys.

Prince Harry

He's the third in line to the British throne . . . and he's been said to be harboring a long-distance crush on Hilary!

Queen's Court, The

In 2003, Hilary briefly considered starring in a feature film from a script with this title, which she described as being like a "teen *Charlie's Angels.*"

Rat fink

This is Hilary's least favorite expression ever—it totally icks her out!

Recke, Andre

The affable music manager who has guided Hilary from her first notes on *Santa Claus Lane* through the present, Andre has had plenty of experience in the industry. He worked on boy-band merchandising (Backstreet's back . . . all right!) in Europe and managed the lovely recording star Myra.

Andre met Hilary at a Radio Disney concert in Anaheim, California, in 2001 and knew right away that she had star potential. He has hooked her up with first-class creative partners like Kara DioGuardi and The Matrix and has overseen all her musical and merchandising decisions.

Andre manages Hilary through Boo Management, but his presence in her professional life is anything but ghostly—he's a rock-solid part of the Hilary Duff Machine . . . and a very nice guy!

Role models

She told a Japanese reporter in 2003 that, "Kids should look up to people that have changed the world, like doctors or astronauts." As a little girl, Hilary admired more commonly idolized people herself, like the *Boy Meets World* cast, Jonathan Taylor Thomas, Spice Girls, and Hanson.

Rome

The Italian capital, where Lizzie McGuire and her classmates took a graduation trip in the lavish *Lizzie McGuire Movie*. The film played up that Italian connection with a soundtrack that included a remake of "Volare" by Vitamin C.

Haylie, Troy, and Hilary en route to the Grammys in 2004!

Rowland, Troy

Starting as Hilary's dialogue coach from the *Lizzie McGuire* days (he appeared as Mr. Lang in four episodes of the series), Troy has been everything from tutor to bodyguard to best buddy to Hilary. He's traveled the globe with her, helped keep her secrets, and given her advice. He is even listed as an associate producer on *Raise Your Voice*! "He knows more than anybody," Hilary says of this warm-hearted, intelligent, fiercely loyal sidekick.

Schedule

Hilary's attitude about her schedule has shifted. On the one hand, when she was younger, she told the press that she loved being busy: "When I'm not working I'm like, 'Oh, God—what am I supposed to do today?' I kind of like the schedule of, 'Okay, I'm going to be here, here, and here. I like that!" But more recently, Hilary has said that while she appreciates non-stop work, she actually likes to be surprised by her daily schedule.

Screen name

No, I'm not giving out Hilary's screen name in this book. But if it makes you feel any better, she's hardly ever on-line. She can't go on-line because "Everybody's got my screen name!" She used to use her dad's screen name and joked that he didn't know how to use a computer anyway!

Shoes

Hilary is a big fan of shoes, and a pair of her signed shoes actually helped raise $2,300 at The 2004 Celebrity Auction for Breast Cancer Research, exceeding the amount raised by a number of other major stars' signed shoes.

Simple Plan

This pop/punk band opened for Hilary on *Hilary Duff's Island Birthday Bash* on The WB. During their stay on Kauai, she became fast friends with the French-Canadian rockers. She's particularly close with David ("She's a great girl. I really think she's a great friend. Any guy would like to hang out with Hilary!"), and phones the guys every chance she gets.

Simpson, Ashlee

Jessica's younger sister attended a Kids With A Cause event in Toronto alongside the Duffs long before she tasted fame as the singer behind 2004's best-selling *Autobiography* CD.

When Ashlee suffered a humiliating lip-synching snafu on *Saturday Night Live,* Hilary responded with loyalty, and offered an insight into her own views on the controversial subject. "I've definitely felt pressure, but the band and me are all live so I feel really comfortable about that—that could never happen to me," Hilary told TeenMusic.com. "But I have felt pressure before because in Europe they want you to lip-synch on their TV shows and it's really hard to stand your ground because there it's so normal. I'm actually friends with Ashlee and people are giving her such a hard time . . . I just think it sucks. There are times when I have trouble singing and I have to just stand there for a second. I think there are always two sides and Ashlee could have been sick or had a bad throat so was told to mime."

The Sims

Hilary's fave video game.

HilaryDuff

Snacks

Hilary is not against snacking—or eating normally, for that matter. No raw-food diets or calorie counting for her. Her athletic metabolism helps her keep fit in spite of snacks like her beloved ice cream or the macadamia-nut-and-chocolate chip cookies she was observed munching at her *Teen Vogue* cover shoot (were they possibly the first cookies ever to be served on a *Teen Vogue* set???). She also digs veggies and is particularly fond of okra.

This is not to say that Hilary has a carefree attitude about her body. She is well aware of the pressures girls feel to stay thin. "Even if I wasn't in this job, I would still worry about it. I'm a normal girl. But I think I've learned to try and not pay too much attention to it."

Spears, Britney

This diva is one of Hilary's favorite artists. "I'm such a big fan of hers—I *love* her!" Hilary has said. La Duff also feels Britney has been too severely criticized for her mistakes, which she chalks up to being young and having fun. "She's such a great entertainer. She gets a lot of flak that she doesn't deserve—I think it's just because . . . people hold her to a higher standard."

The affection is mutual. At my interview with her at the Château Marmont in 2003, Britney said of Hilary, "Me and my girlfriend were watching *Making the Video* and it was her video that came on. She is completely just a light to the world. She is so beautiful and so incredibly sweet. My little sister is completely in love with her. I'm a big fan of hers! She is just a doll. I don't think she needs advice! I think she's doing pretty darn good. Her song ["So Yesterday"] is amazing and she has her whole little cool clothes thing going on, her cute little outfits, and her personality is amazing—so I don't think she needs advice. Maybe, if anything, just be herself and never change!"

One thing Britney's famous for is revealing clothing, something Hilary won't be embracing anytime soon. "Well, everyone keeps saying to me, 'Uh-oh, what, are you gonna take your clothes off or something now?'" But Hilary has said she firmly believes that you don't have to show your body to look good.

Surfing

Decked out in a bikini, Hilary learned to surf in a single afternoon while filming her TV special on Kauai in Hawaii—and she learned from the best! Teen surf pro Shaun White personally coached Hilary on how to hang ten!

Techno

Hil's least fave musical genre is techno—it gives her a headache.

Teenager of the Year

No less an authority than *Rolling Stone* proclaimed Hil to be the Teenager of the Year for 2003!

Touring

In 2002, Hilary was very nervous about touring live. She got her feet wet doing radio shows, then plunged into an extensive *Metamorphosis* Tour in 2003 and her well-received, even more geographically ambitious *Most Wanted* Tour in 2004. "I had no idea how much work it takes to put on a tour—not just for me, but for everybody!" Hilary told *Pollstar* after she'd made some appearances. Live, Hilary eschews choreographed dance moves in favor of a looser, rock-style stage stalk—she's less Britney, more Avril, and all Hilary.

Tricks

Two of Hilary's hidden talents include doing yo-yo stunts and being able to walk on her hands!

Tyler, Steven

He's the outrageous Aerosmith lead singer who made an appearance on a very cool *Lizzie McGuire* Christmas episode. He has a thing for Hilary, as the baffled pop star discovered. "At the *mtvICON* show for Aerosmith, Steven Tyler was like, 'Hilary, dude, I'm so excited you're here—I love you!'" she told *CosmoGirl!* breathlessly. "I thought it was weird, but then someone asked me, 'You didn't know you were Steven's special guest?'"

Vancouver

City in Canada where Hilary filmed parts of *Agent Cody Banks*.

Vanity Fair

Thanks to the tween boom, Hilary Duff and a handful of her peers made it to the cover of this legendary general-interest magazine together long before they might have on their own; specifically, in July of 2003. The main cover featured (from left to right) Amanda Bynes, the Olsen twins, Mandy Moore, and Hilary, and the fold-out cover continued on to feature Alexis Bledel, Evan Rachel Wood, Raven-Symoné, and Lindsay Lohan. Inside, the issue's lengthy story on male and female teen idols featured quirky commentary on all of these girls and other stars, including Solange Knowles, Brittany Snow, Aaron Meeks, the *Harry Potter* actors, Bow Wow, Shia LaBeouf, Aaron Carter, Lacey Chabert, Kaley Cuoco, AJ Trauth, Milo Ventimiglia, Jared Padalecki, Frankie Muniz, Kyla Pratt, Alexa Vega, Emily Van Camp, and Christina Milian.

The April 27, 2003, photo shoot at Smashbox Studios in Culver City, California, required Hilary and Lindsay to pillow-fight on a bed . . . which would have been fine, except Hilary invited her boyfriend Aaron Carter to visit, despite his history with Lindsay. The situation was not as pretty as the cover wound up being—and Hilary is arguably the focal point of that cover.

In the article, Hilary confesses to owning "probably together over a dozen" Juicy Couture outfits, brings up longtime crush David Beckham, professes a love for *I Dream of Jeannie*, and decries "chipped nail polish and wastefulness." Her pet peeve is "people who drink half a can of soda and leave to get another one because they can't remember where they put the first one."

Venice Beach

This kooky, colorful, Cali hotspot is where Hilary lensed her "So Yesterday" video. Scenes happened all along the boardwalk (where she happily signed autographs for disbelieving fans and posed for a pic with a cute button salesman) and on the beach. If you travel there, you will still find the Vincent Van Gogh–inspired wall where some of the action took place.

VideoNow

Thanks to a deal with Hasbro, Hilary released a special minifilm called *A Day in the Life of Hilary Duff* in July 2003 for the popular VideoNow system.

"What Christmas Should Be"

Hil sang this song, from the updated 2003 rerelease of her *Santa Claus Lane* CD, at the 2004 Christmas tree lighting at Rockefeller Center in New York City.

"You rock!"

One of Hilary's pet phrases, she says it more often than some teenage girls say "um" and "like." She particularly loves to say it to her fans at concerts.

Zoe

This is the fake name Hilary likes to use when traveling to maintain her privacy. I'll keep to myself the fake last name she uses. . . .

Workography

A Complete Listing
of All of
Hilary's Projects!

MOVIES!

Playing by Heart (Miramax, R)
    Director: Willard Carroll
    Theatrical Release: December 30, 1998
    DVD Release: February 4, 2003
    Budget: $14 million
    Domestic Gross: $3,970,078
    Character: Uncredited

This movie was originally entitled *Dancing About Architecture*, which is from the phrase, "Talking about love is like dancing about architecture." This complex relationship film was released in December 1998 in order to capture some Oscar gold, but critics were not sufficiently wowed and audiences agreed.

One impressive thing about this overlooked film is its monumental cast! Hilary is merely an extra, but she appears in a movie with everyone you can think of: Sean Connery, Angelina Jolie, Gena Rowlands, Ryan Phillippe, Gillian Anderson, Ellen Burstyn, Dennis Quaid, Patricia Clarkson, Anthony Edwards, Madeleine Stowe, Jon Stewart, and Jay Mohr!

Human Nature (Fine Line, R)
    Director: Michel Gondry
    Theatrical Release: April 12, 2002
    DVD Release: June 1, 2004
    Budget: Unknown
    Domestic Gross: $705,308
    Character: Young Lila Jute

Before Hilary became a teen star, she took parts in R-rated films with artistic merit like this Sundance and Cannes Film Festival favorite.

The plot is bizarre! A scientist (Tim Robbins) and his girlfriend (Patricia Arquette) discover a man raised in the wild (Rhys Ifans). They fight over whether to let him keep his animalistic freedom or to help him adapt to the more civilized world of humans.

One major plot element is that Patricia Arquette's character, Lila Jute, has an almost surreal body-hair problem. Hilary plays the young Lila, so we see Hil at her hairiest!

This is not exactly the kind of movie to rent for that sleepover you're planning, but it provides an early glimpse of Hilary's acting talents—she does "distraught" very well on film!

Besides getting to work with Patricia Arquette and Tim Robbins, Hilary was acting in a film written by Charlie Kaufman, whose brilliant

Hilary Duff

screenplays for *Being John Malkovich, Adaptation, Confessions of a Dangerous Mind,* and *Eternal Sunshine of the Spotless Mind* would make him one of the decade's hottest talents.

Agent Cody Banks (MGM, PG)

Director: Harald Zwart
Theatrical Release: March 14, 2003
DVD Release: August 5, 2003
Budget: $28 million
Domestic Gross: $47,938,330
Character: Natalie Connors

Hilary's first major movie role was as a girl in danger (Natalie Connors, though the character's name was changed many times before filming commenced) in this teen James Bond flick, starring real-life friend Frankie Muniz in the title role.

Amusingly, skateboarding whiz Cody is groomed by the CIA as a world-class spy while dealing with middle school. His big mission is to make friends with the beautiful Natalie to get closer to her dad, a scientist who is unwittingly aiding an evil world-domination organization.

There's plenty of action along the way, including car chases and spectacular stunts that both Hilary and Frankie loved.

Hilary generally denies dating Frankie in real life, though in *Interview* magazine she did acknowledge dating him briefly when she was directly asked by Taylor Hanson. It seems if they did date, it wasn't very memorable—not as memorable as this eye-popping thrill ride of a movie. The *Los Angeles Times* noted that the film "may be targeted at teens, but even their grandparents might consider it fun."

Agent Cody Banks spawned a sequel, *Agent Cody Banks 2: Destination London,* but the pretty blond in that movie was Hannah Spearritt, not Hilary Duff.

Agent Cody Banks Trivia!

• Producer Dylan Sellers says the idea to cast Hilary Duff came from his daughter, Natalie Sellers, who told him to get "that girl from *Lizzie McGuire*!" She was rewarded by having Hilary's character named after her!

• Jennifer Love Hewitt was originally cast to play the dangerously sexy Ronica Miles, but the part eventually went to Angie Harmon!

• Hilary first heard about this project when Frankie guest starred on *Lizzie McGuire*!

• Major *Malcolm in the Middle* superstar Frankie was paid $2 million for this role, and newcomer Hilary received a hefty quarter of that amount and got her name above the title!

• Among the producers on this movie are the famous names Jason Alexander (*Seinfeld*) and Madonna!

The Lizzie McGuire Movie (Buena Vista, PG)
Director: Jim Fall
Theatrical Release: May 2, 2003
DVD Release: August 12, 2003
Budget: $17 million
Domestic Gross: $42,734,455
Character: Elizabeth Brooke McGuire

It's only fitting that Hilary's first starring role in a major motion picture would be as Lizzie McGuire—after a successful run on TV, she was paid a million dollars to re-create the role for the big screen. Originally titled *Ciao, Lizzie!*, the movie was announced at the same time a for-TV-only *Even Stevens* movie was announced.

In *The Lizzie McGuire Movie*, Lizzie, Gordo (Adam Lamberg), Kate (Ashlie Brillault), Ethan (Clayton Snyder), and their whole class go on a two-week middle-school graduation trip to Italy, or "the land where they invented spaghetti," as Ethan would say. Hey, it was either that or a thirty-six-hour bus ride to Waterslide Wonderland!

On impact, Lizzie is mistaken for Isabella (also played by Hilary), a glamorous Italian pop star. Isabella is on strike, so her singing partner Paolo (Yani Gellman) is desperate to replace her—but is he being nice to Lizzie because he genuinely likes her, or is he sucking up just to get Lizzie to impersonate Isabella and help him save face?

The movie could be read as a pre–Ashlee Simpson on *Saturday Night Live* sermon against lip-synching (Paolo claims Isabella mimes their songs, but it turns out to be Paolo who is the fraud), or it could be read as an acting-out of Hilary and Aaron Carter's dating history ("You guys are definitely broken up, right?" Lizzie asks Paolo), but most of all it's the exact movie *Lizzie McGuire* fans always dreamed of.

From the opening, where we see Lizzie rockin' out to Atomic Kitten's "The Tide Is High (Get the Feeling)," the movie truly captures the spirit of the series. Fans also get to see a long-awaited smooch between Lizzie and Gordo, which was the one scene Hilary sweated out in advance—"It's like kissing your brother!" she told the director.

The climax comes with Lizzie performing live onstage in a clear try-out for Hilary's real-life metamorphosis from actress to pop star! Even if you don't think this is Hilary's best movie ever, it's definitely one that her fans will always consider a special treat to watch.

The Lizzie McGuire Movie

Miniquiz!

1. What famous playwright does Lizzie's dad quote before she takes off for Italy?

. . . .

2. Who accuses Lizzie of being an "outfit repeater"?

. . . .

3. Name the class valedictorian who fails to make the trip.

. . . .

4. How many "historically significant Roman landmarks" does Ms. Ungermeyer (Alex Borstein) claim the class will see in two weeks?

. . . .

5. What gift does the plump fan give Lizzie when she mistakes her for Isabella?

. . . .

Answers
1. William Shakespeare
2. Kate Sanders (Ashlie Brillault)
3. Margaret Chan
4. Thirty-one
5. "Some cool cheese."

Hilary Duff

Classic Quotes!

"Some say juvenile . . . I say genius!"

—Jake Thomas, *The Lizzie McGuire Movie*

"How famous do you have to be before you need a bodyguard?"

—Hilary Duff, *The Lizzie McGuire Movie*

"Jewelry—now that's a language every girl understands!"

—Hilary Duff, *The Lizzie McGuire Movie*

"Diva—good. Tacky—bad."

—Hilary Duff, *The Lizzie McGuire Movie*

"Good-bye, Lizzie McGuire, hello, fabulous!"

—Hilary Duff, *The Lizzie McGuire Movie*

The Lizzie McGuire Movie Trivia!

• The first scene filmed, on October 14, 2002, was the scene in Rome where Lizzie hops on the Vespa with Paolo!

• "What Dreams Are Made Of" was written by Dean Pitchford, who also wrote "Footloose" and won an Oscar and a Golden Globe for writing "Fame"!

• Originally, there was a roller-skating scene planned for a location in Rome. Unfortunately, the site was a tomb . . . so that scene got scratched!

• The director, Jim Fall, never heard of *Lizzie McGuire* before he was offered the movie!

• Italy wasn't the only country outside the USA where *The Lizzie McGuire Movie* was filmed—the movie was also shot in Canada!

Cheaper by the Dozen (20th Century Fox, PG)

Director: Shawn Levy

Theatrical Release: December 25, 2003

DVD Release: August 31, 2004

Budget: $40 million

Domestic Gross: $138,614,544

Character: Lorraine Baker

"This Christmas the More . . . the Scarier!" was the tagline used to promote this blockbuster about the Bakers, a family from a tiny town in Illinois who move to the big city when the dad (Steve Martin) gets a shot at coaching the football team of his alma mater. The catches are that there are twelve kids in this family and that the mother (Bonnie Hunt) is missing in action thanks to a book promo tour.

Essentially a simple comedy of errors, *Cheaper by the Dozen* benefited from opening on Christmas Day, drawing in huge crowds hungry for family fare. Parents were excited by the major grown-up stars and kids were eager to see Hilary (even though as Lorraine Baker she plays a very small supporting role), Ashton Kutcher (who steals the movie but whose role is uncredited), and *Smallville* hunk Tom Welling (playing a teenager for the last time ever, we're guessing).

Before *Cheaper by the Dozen* was released, Hilary described it this way: "I just finished a movie with this huge ensemble cast and it was fun because it was like Steve Martin, Bonnie Hunt, Piper Perabo, Tom Welling, Ashton Kutcher . . . lots of really cool people in that!"

Cheaper by the Dozen Set Secret!

Hilary ran into a bit of trouble with Ashton Kutcher during the making of this box-office hit!

"I met Ashton Kutcher on the set of *Cheaper by the Dozen*," she told *CosmoGirl!* magazine. "He's such a goofball! At The MTV Movie Awards, while I was presenting, I said onstage that Colin Farrell was hotter than him. So when I saw Ashton the next day, he said, 'You think *he's* hotter? You're going to get it!' I don't know what he'll do—but I can tell you, I'm scared!"

As we all know, Ashton later goofed on Hilary on his MTV show *Punk'd* to playfully pay her back. Now you know why her targeted her!

A Cinderella Story (Warner Bros., PG)

Director: Mark Rosman

Theatrical Release: July 16, 2004

DVD Release: October 19, 2004

Budget: $19 million

Domestic Gross: $51,431,160

Character: Samantha Martin

Probably Hilary's fans' fave flick of hers, this adorable romantic comedy has just enough tragedy to allow Hilary to show off her dramatic acting abilities. The story begins with Samantha "Sam" Martin (Hilary) losing her beloved dad in an earthquake. Due to his unfortunate taste in women, she is left to be raised by a modern-day wicked stepmother, plastic surgery buff Fiona (Jennifer Coolidge), and forced to cater to two ugly-even-on-the-inside stepsisters, Brianna and Gabriella (Madeline Zima and Andrea Avery).

Sam struggles as a waitress at the family diner, guided by Rhonda (Regina King), whose wisdom and affection for Sam make her an effective fairy godmother.

At school, Sam is *not* popular. She hangs out with her buddy Carter (Dan Byrd) and exists under the radar of the cool crowd . . . until her cell phone falls into the hands of Austin Ames (Chad Michael Murray), the cutest guy in school. They begin an anonymous correspondence that will end with a most improbable and sigh-inducing fairy-tale ending.

While this movie was being made, there was an unusual amount of speculation about the cast! Rupert Grint was rumored to be signed, as was Carmen Rasmussen of *American Idol* fame.

**Open Your Eyes
for This
"Our Lips Are Sealed"
On-Set Peek!**

This gorgeous "Jeux Jaloux" mirror
was destroyed during the filming!

Hil and Hay bundle up in the
cold Toronto wind!

A behind-the-scenes peek at video director Chris Applebaum at work!

The girls have to run like crazy to finish this shot in time!

The entire _A Cinderella Story_ film and "Our Lips Are Sealed" video sets were strictly closed . . . except to photographer Keith Munyan!

Interview with Hilary Duff: The Making of *A Cinderella Story*!

Matthew: *How was it filming* A Cinderella Story?

Hilary: It was really, really fun. I got to work with Jennifer Coolidge, who is like an idol of mine! She's awesome and she's brilliant to watch. I could just watch her facial expressions all day long. The stuff that she comes up with and uses with the material and the acting and stuff is incredible—she is so brilliant. I loved working with her—she's hilarious. And Regina King is really great. And I had fun working with Chad. . . .

Matthew: *[Kidding] Is he princely or more of a frog?*

Hilary: Ahhh! Matthew, that's *horrible!* [Laughs] That's so funny. He's princely because he plays the prince. We got along really well, the whole cast, and Chad and I started going places together just hanging out and being friends and, like, *everyone* started talking about it. We're like, "Can't do *that* anymore."

Matthew: *I thought it was weird that you were reported to be dating, but then the press didn't even point out that if you were dating, you're only fifteen and he's over twenty!*

Hilary: I know! It's like people don't realize I'm fifteen and he's twenty-two and *that* wouldn't be happening. We went to a couple of places together like WB parties because we were working together.

Matthew: *How was it playing a character who's so different from all the others you've played so far?*

Hilary: It was really challenging. I had a hard time because—I mean, *you* know all the projects that I've done I've been, like, really into clothes and hair and makeup and I've gotten to be a lot of who I am, and in this movie I had to totally build this character, which Troy [Rowland] really helped me out with a lot because he's my dialogue coach. I built this character that I've never had to relate to because nothing like that has ever happened to me before.

The character was always being told how ugly she is and how she'll never be anything else but a busboy working at the diner and everyone at school makes fun of her and she's had a really tough life.

It was definitely hard, but it was nice to have the whole *metamorphosis* in the movie!

Chad Michael Murray: Get to Know "Austin Ames"

Chad Michael Murray—or The Chad as he was dubbed on the *Freaky Friday* set—is that rare actor who has worked with both Lindsay Lohan and Hilary Duff and remained on good terms with both. Who is this laid-back California dude? Well, for starters, he's a North Carolinian as long as he's the star of The WB's *One Tree Hill*, which shoots in Wilmington.

Before he was the number-one attraction on the cover of every teen magazine, Chad was an actor who did everything from *Dawson's Creek* to *Gilmore Girls* and a failed pilot for *The Lone Ranger*. Even then, he seemed to be kickin' back and waiting for fame to catch up to him!

When asked by *Popstar!* what embarrasses him, he said quickly, "Not much."

In high school, Chad was less Austin and more Carter . . . read: not one of the cool kids!

Here, Chad looks like a rebellious "Mr. James Dean," but Hilary knows this heartthrob has a heart of gold!

"I went to Clarence High in Buffalo and I couldn't stand it. I liked the educational part . . . but man, the second that bell rang, I had to deal with this kid and that kid and . . . yeah, I was a nerd!"

Over the years, he developed—thanks in part to his natural athleticism and healthy living—into a total hottie, armed with great advice on how to charm girls!

"My dad just said to be sweet, kind, and courteous, and the trick is opening the doors, paying for dinner, and making them feel like they're the greatest thing in the world."

Sounds like his fiancée, Sophia Bush (his costar on *One Tree Hill*, who has taken to wearing a shirt with "Feyoncé" on it), is living her own Cinderella story right about now!

Now if only we can get Chad and Hilary to team up again in another great movie!

interview

Raise Your Voice (New Line, PG)
    Director: Sean Patrick McNamara
    Theatrical Release: October 8, 2004
    DVD Release: February 15, 2005
    Budget: $14 million
    Domestic Gross: $10,411,980
    Character: Terri Fletcher

This bittersweet tale follows young Terri Fletcher (Hilary) as she leaves her overprotective dad's small-town home to attend a prestigious and highly competitive summer music academy called Bristol-Hillman in Los Angeles.

Terri only got into the school because, unbeknownst to her, her brother Paul (Jason Ritter) had made and submitted to the staff a DVD showing off his sister's talents, her personality, and her "amazing voice." Sadly, Paul was killed when a drunk driver hit the car in which the siblings were traveling home from a Three Days Grace concert.

Inspired by her brother's faith, Terri nervously stands up to the many challenges at the school, from a sassy roommate (Dana Davis) to a lovestruck romeo (Oliver James) to musical training that pushes her voice to its limits. *Raise Your Voice* is an old-school coming-of-age movie with plenty of musical interludes, including the songs "Someone's Watching Over Me," "Jericho," and "Fly," all of which appear on Hilary's *Hilary Duff* CD.

Originally, the film was entitled *Heart of Summer* and Ashlee Simpson was listed in the early cast credits.

Years before *Raise Your Voice* was made, Jim Fall was attached to direct it and he auditioned a promising newcomer named Haylie Duff. He had to bow out when he was offered *The Lizzie McGuire Movie* starring Hilary Duff. You know what happened next . . . small world!

Raise Your Voice contains performances by a slew of well-known actors, including Rita Wilson, Rebecca DeMornay, John Corbett, David Keith, and Johnny Lewis of the TV show *Quintuplets*.

The Perfect Man (Universal, PG)

   Director: Mark Rosman
   Theatrical Release: August 12, 2005
   DVD Release: 2005
   Budget: $20 million
   Character: Holly Hamilton

For this heart-tugging and smile-stretching romantic comedy, Hilary teams up again with her *Cinderella Story* director, Mark Rosman. The story follows a young girl, Holly (Hilary), who is trying to play matchmaker for her single mother (Heather Locklear). The movie is based on the real-life story of screenwriter Heather Robinson, who got into trouble with authorities over her unorthodox methods of trying to hook up her mom with true love!

   Sex and the City's Big (Chris Noth) and *Queer Eye for the Straight Guy*'s Carson Kressley are along for the ride in what promises to be a big hit for Hil—and a fan-pleasing take on *Sleepless in Seattle*!

Upcoming Movies:

Material Girls (Maverick) costarring Haylie Duff in 2005 or 2006, and *Outward Blonde* in 2006.

Hilary Duff

Classic Quotes!

"Call me a dork, but I love choir practice!"

—Hilary Duff, *Raise Your Voice*

"Music is a higher revelation than all wisdom and philosophy."

—Ludwig van Beethoven, as quoted in *Raise Your Voice*

"Haven't you ever heard of making your own luck?"

—Hilary Duff, *Raise Your Voice*

Raise Your Voice

Miniquiz!

1. Name the fake TV show Terri's brother is making . . . then name the show Terri jokingly says he must be making considering he's shooting footage of *her*.

. . . .

2. Who wins the scholarship at the end?

. . . .

3. Name the establishment where Terri and Jay attempt some karaoke.

. . . .

4. What song do the teens sing at the fountain?

. . . .

5. What is Kiwi's real first name?

. . . .

Answers

1. *The Fletcher Experience* and *America's Most Boring Teenagers*
2. Denise Gilmore (Dana Davis)
3. The Blue Moon
4. "The Way You Do the Things You Do"
5. Engelbert

Music!

Studio CDs!

Santa Claus Lane **(Buena Vista Records)**

Released: October 15, 2002

Reissued: October 14, 2003

Certified: 500,000+

1. "What Christmas Should Be"
2. "Santa Claus Lane"
3. "Santa Claus Is Coming to Town"
4. "I Heard Santa on the Radio" duet with Christina Milian
5. "Jingle Bell Rock"
6. "When the Snow Comes Down in Tinseltown"
7. "Sleigh Ride"
8. "Tell Me a Story (About the Night Before)" duet with Lil' Romeo
9. "Last Christmas"
10. "Same Old Christmas" by Haylie Duff
11. "Wonderful Christmas Time"

The reissued version contains the extra song "What Christmas Should Be" as the first track.

Metamorphosis **(Hollywood Records)**

Released: August 26, 2003

Shipped: 800,000+

Certified: 3,000,000+

Debut: Number two (204,000 sold first week)

Peak Position: Number one

1. "So Yesterday"
2. "Come Clean"
3. "Workin' It Out"
4. "Little Voice"
5. "Where Did I Go Right?"
6. "Anywhere but Here"
7. "The Math"
8. "Love Just Is"
9. "Sweet Sixteen"
10. "Party Up"
11. "Metamorphosis"
12. "Inner Strength"
13. "Why Not"

"Girl Can Rock" is a Target exclusive bonus track and that song plus "A Day in the Sun" are bonuses on Asian imports.

Hilary Duff (Hollywood Records)

Released: September 28, 2004

Shipped: 1,000,000+

Certified: 2,000,000+

Debut: Number two (192,000 sold first week)

Peak Position: Number two

1. "Fly"
2. "Do You Want Me?"
3. "Weird"
4. "Hide Away"
5. "Mr. James Dean"
6. "Underneath This Smile"
7. "Dangerous to Know"
8. "Who's That Girl?"
9. "Shine"
10. "I Am"
11. "The Getaway"
12. "Cry"
13. "Haters"
14. "Rock This World"
15. "Someone's Watching Over Me"
16. "Jericho"
17. "The Last Song"

Bonus tracks on Asian imports are "Who's That Girl?" (acoustic mix), "My Generation," and "Our Lips Are Sealed" with Haylie Duff.

Selected Compilation CDs!

The Lizzie McGuire Soundtrack (Buena Vista Records)
    Released: August 13, 2002
    Certified: Platinum
The first album to contain vocals by Hilary Duff features her song "I Can't Wait."

The Lizzie McGuire Movie Soundtrack (Walt Disney Records)
    Released: April 22, 2003
    Certified: Platinum
This album contains "Why Not" (both the regular mix and a special McMix) and "What Dreams Are Made Of" (ballad and regular versions) by Hilary Duff, as well as "Girl in the Band" by Haylie Duff.

Disneymania (Walt Disney Records)
    Released: September 17, 2002
This Disney compilation has Hilary's "The Tiki, Tiki Room."

Disneymania 2 (Walt Disney Records)
    Released: January 27, 2004
The *Disneymania* sequel features Hilary and Haylie Duff's duet on "The Siamese Cat Song" as well as Hilary's vocals as part of Disney Channel's Circle of Stars on "Circle of Life."

A Cinderella Story Soundtrack (Hollywood Records)
    Released: July 13, 2004
Among its fourteen tracks is the Haylie Duff song "One in This World," the "Our Lips Are Sealed" duet between Hilary and Haylie, and the following Hilary Duff songs: "Crash World," "Now You Know," "Girl Can Rock," and "Anywhere but Here." A Target exclusive bonus track is "Metamorphosis (Live)."

Thanks and Giving All Year Long (Rhino Records)
    Released: November 16, 2004
Hilary's "(I'll Give) Anything but Up!" appears on this charming CD, which is the musical companion to actress Marlo Thomas's Thanksgiving book of the same name.

DVDs!

Casper Meets Wendy (20th Century Fox)
Director: Sean McNamara
Released: September 22, 1998
Reissued: September 7, 2004
Character: Wendy

Hilary's first leading role was in this made-for-video release. It was so popular that it was rereleased in 2004.

Hilary Duff: All Access Pass (Universal Music and Video)
Released: November 4, 2003

Including the rare videos for "I Can't Wait," "Why Not," and also "So Yesterday," this compilation also offers the making of two of those vid clips and the recording of *Metamorphosis*.

Hilary Duff: The Concert—The Girl Can Rock (Buena Vista Home Video)
Released: August 10, 2004

This compilation offers concert footage, behind-the-scenes features, the "So Yesterday" and "Come Clean" videos, and an interview with Ryan Seacrest.

Hilary Duff: Learning to Fly (Universal Music and Video)
Released: November 16, 2004

This DVD contains the making of and the final version of the "Fly" video, introduces Hilary's band and crew, and offers the complete video. It also shows behind-the-scenes moments from her *Most Wanted* Tour.

TV Series!

Lizzie McGuire (Disney Channel)
  First Airdate: January 19, 2001
  Last Airdate: February 14, 2004
  Character: Elizabeth Brooke McGuire

Hilary has come a long way from her *Lizzie McGuire* days, but there's no denying the sugary perfection of her debut series. Hilary played the title character, an endearingly awkward girl next door who survived every mortal embarrassment from class picture day, parties, school plays, bad acting (best friend Miranda's in *Greasier*), and her brother/sister (or is it a crush?) friendship with Gordo. Exactly sixty-five episodes were filmed, only about three years' worth of shows, and yet it continues in reruns on Disney Channel, a surefire bet to become the *Brady Bunch* for Hilary's generation!

TV Movies and Miniseries!

True Women (CBS)
  Director: Karen Arthur
  First Airdate: May 18, 1997
  DVD Release: August 20, 2002
  Character: Uncredited
Civil War drama abut women struggling against the odds.

The Soul Collector (CBS)
  Director: Michael Scott
  First Airdate: October 24, 1999
  DVD Release: Unavailable
  Character: Ellie
Spiritually charged movie about an angel's good deed on Earth.

Cadet Kelly (Disney Channel/ABC)
  Director: Larry Shaw
  First Airdate: March 8, 2002/July 14, 2002
  DVD Release: Unavailable
  Character: Kelly Collins
Hilary's physically draining role about a spoiled girl taking on military school—and winning.

Selected TV Guest Appearances!

Chicago Hope (CBS) "Cold Hearts"
> **First Airdate: March 30, 2000**
> **Character: Jessie Seldon**

Hilary plays a desperately ill child in this heart tugger of a drama.

George Lopez (ABC) "Team Leader"
> **First Airdate: April 30, 2003**
> **Character: Stephanie**

A relatively brief and light appearance as a schoolgirl.

Punk'd (MTV) Season 2, Episode 9
> **First Airdate: October 26, 2003**
> **Character: Herself**

Hilary gets fooled by Ashton Kutcher. She wasn't mad, but it did rob her of precious time she had set aside to do driver's training!

American Dreams (NBC) "Change a-Comin'"
> **First Airdate: November 23, 2003**
> **Character: The Shangri-Las (with Haylie Duff)**

The sisters team up to portray '60s singing act the Shangri-Las.

Frasier (NBC) "Frasier-Lite"
> **First Airdate: January 6, 2004**
> **Character: Voice of Britney**

Hilary is never seen in one of the last episodes of this classic series.

Kids on Deck (YES) Multiple appearances
> **First Airdate: May 16, 2004**
> **Character: Herself**

Hilary appears in vignettes designed to teach kids about baseball.

Joan of Arcadia (CBS) "Unknown"
> **First Airdate: February 4, 2005**
> **Character: Unknown**

Hilary will appear on the show alongside *Raise Your Voice* costar Jason Ritter.

Bibliography

Billboard, "Hilary Duff: A Performer's Metamorphosis" (January 26, 2004), by Craig Rosen.

Billboard, "Hilary Duff . . . Teen Star Takes Advantage of Branding Opportunities" (July 5, 2003), by Steve Traiman.

Blender, "Good Girls Don't . . . But She Does! Have Hit Records, Movies and TV Shows, That Is . . ." (October 2004), by Nick Duerden.

CosmoGirl!, "CG! Catches Up with . . . Hilary Duff" (October 2003), by Lauren Brown.

Cowboys & Indians, "Hilary Duff: A Texas Metamorphosis" (June 2004), by William C. Reynolds.

Hangin' with Hilary Duff (Scholastic, 2003), by Jo Hurley.

Hilary Duff: A Not-So-Typical Teen (Simon & Schuster Spotlight, 2003), by Nancy Krulik.

Hilary Duff: Actress and Singer (Mitchell Lane, 2005), by Marylou Morano Kjelle.

Hilary Duff: Style, Fashion, Guys and More! (Triumph, 2004), by Mary Boone.

Hilary Duff: Total Hilary, Metamorphosis, Lizzie McGuire, *and More!* (Triumph, 2003), by Mary Boone.

Hilary Rocks: On Stage and Screen, and in Between, Hilary Duff Living a Fairy Tale Life (Triumph, 2004), by Mary Boone.

Hollywood Reporter, "Hilary Duff Lands Major Movies"(March 26, 2002).

In Touch Weekly, "Is It True?" and "Too Much, Too Soon?" (September 1, 2003).

Interview, "Hilary Duff" (February 2004), by Taylor Hanson.

"Life Story: Hilary Duff—A Keepsake Edition Dedicated to This Real-Life Cinderella!" (Bauer, 2004).

"Life Story: Hilary Duff—America's #1 Teen Star!" (Bauer, 2004).

"Life Story: Hilary Duff—Step Inside Her Fairy Tale World!" (Bauer, 2004).

"Life Story: Hilary Duff—The Ultimate Tribute to America's Sweetheart!" (Bauer, 2004).

MSN chat (December 2002).

The National Enquirer, "Look Out Britney! Here Comes 'Lizzie McGuire'" (May 16, 2002), by Beverly Williston and Rick Egusquiza.

The National Enquirer, "Hilary Duff's Mom Chases Down Suspect in Stalker Drama!" (August 25, 2003), by Beverly Williston and Jim Nelson.

New Weekly, "Hilary Duff, the Talented U.S. Teenager Singer" (Australia, 2004).

The New York Times, "How Hilary Duff Made Off with Your Daughter" (April 28, 2003), by Hillary Frey.

People Weekly, "Teen Titans" (August 25, 2003).

Popstar! (issues August 2001–April 2005) by Kelly Bryant, Rachel Chang, Izumi Hasegawa, Bob Jamieson, Rana Meyer, and Matthew Rettenmund. All full-length interviews © Matthew Rettenmund reproduced with written permission. To order back issues or to subscribe to *Popstar!*, visit popstaronline.com or AOL Keyword: KOL Popstar, or call 1-866-539-5624.

Rolling Stone, "Teenager of the Year" (September 18, 2003), by Mark Binelli.

Teen Vogue, "Hilary Duff" (December 2004/January 2005), by Lauren Waterman.

USA Today, "Just Can't Get Enough of Duff" (July 15, 2003), by Bruce Horovitz.

USA Today, "Sisters Share Name, Not Fame" (January 8, 2004), by Donna Freydkin.

Vanity Fair, "Teen Engines: Riding with the Kid Culture" (July 2003), by James Wolcott and Krista Smith.

Vanity Fair, "The Tween Queen" (April 2003).

Variety, "What's Lizzie Thinking?—Review" (January 16, 2001), by Laura Fries.

Wall Street Journal, "'Lizzie' Poses a Dilemma for Disney and Duff" (May 6, 2003), by Bruce Orwall.

YM, "On the Verge: Hilary Duff" (May 2003), by Ali Gazan.

Hilary Duff

Official Hilary Site

HilaryDuff.com

Unofficial Hilary Sites

Hilary-Duff.net

HilaryDuff.org

HilaryFan.com

HilaryPix.com

Other Sites

AccessHollywood.com

Amazon.com

AOL Keyword: KOL Popstar

IMDB.com

kidswithacause.com

LaughingPlace.com

Popstaronline.com

Target.com

TeenMusic.com

TVTome.com

Acknowledgments

There are many people I would like to thank for their help in creating this valentine to Hilary Duff for her fans!

Among them, I must thank my partner, José, and my family and friends for their support as I compiled this book over a long period of time. I would also like to thank Kelly Bryant, Rachel Chang, and Rana Meyer, all of whom have worked at *Popstar!* magazine with me and share my enthusiasm for Hilary as a pop-culture phenomenon, and Izumi Hasegawa of *U.S. Frontline*, Bob Jamieson and Renee Rodrigues, whose interviews in *Popstar!* with Hilary I referred to during my research. Thanks also to Jeremy Sperber for some crucial fact-checking help.

I extend my heartfelt thanks to the many people who shared their comments on Hilary Duff to help round out this story, including Karen Bradford, Jim Fall, and Chris Garlington.

I am indebted to both my agent, Danielle Egan-Miller, and her staff, and to my editor Samantha Mandor, without whose vision this book would not exist.

Most of all, I'm very grateful to the kind and generous Susan Duff. Ever since meeting her, she has been unfailingly warm toward me, granting me access unlike any she has given any other writer, even giving me her blessings to do this book. I thank you, Susan, for the hilarious conversations we've shared, for trusting me, and for some of the best non-Hilary Hollywood gossip I've ever heard—you always know the real deal! Thanks also to Bob and Haylie, who have been so open and friendly on the occasions we've met.

And finally, this book is dedicated to its subject, the amazing Hilary Duff, who would, I'm sure, blush to read it. Hilary, keep doing what makes you happy because it obviously makes countless other people just as happy. Continue being "a ray of light to the world," as Britney Spears once called you, and never stop being yourself.

In the words of someone very cool: "You rock!"

—Matthew Rettenmund

I want to thank Susan Duff for allowing me to become part of Hilary's family. It's been a joy and pleasure to photograph Hilary and Haylie over the past two years. From the first day I met Hilary to the present, she has remained the same sweet Texas girl everyone loves. She's a true professional in every sense and will always be the ultimate Barbie to me!

—Keith Munyan

About the Author

Hilary Duff

Matthew Rettenmund (mattrett@aol.com) is the founding editor-in-chief of Popstar! magazine and is the author of the books Encyclopedia Madonnica and Totally Awesome '80s. He has appeared on MTV, VH1, and E! as a pop-culture expert. He lives and works in New York City.

About the Photographer

Keith Munyan is a commercial photographer whose work has appeared in many national magazines. He lives and works in Los Angeles. You can visit his website at www.keithmunyan.com.